# STUDENT UNIT GUIDE

## NEW EDITION

## AQA AS/A2 Biology Units 3 and 6
## Investigative and Practical Skills in Biology

Steve Potter and Martin Rowland

PHILIP ALLAN

Philip Allan, an imprint of Hodder Education, an Hachette UK company, Market Place, Deddington, Oxfordshire OX15 0SE

*Orders*

Bookpoint Ltd, 130 Milton Park, Abingdon, Oxfordshire OX14 4SB
tel: 01235 827827
fax: 01235 400401
e-mail: education@bookpoint.co.uk
Lines are open 9.00 a.m.–5.00 p.m., Monday to Saturday, with a 24-hour message answering service.
You can also order through the Philip Allan Updates website: www.philipallan.co.uk

© Steve Potter and Martin Rowland 2012

ISBN 978-1-4441-7861-6

First printed 2012
Impression number 5 4 3 2 1
Year 2017 2016 2015 2014 2013 2012

Cover photo: Fotolia

Typeset by Integra Software Services Pvt. Ltd., Pondicherry, India

Printed in Dubai

Hachette UK's policy is to use papers that are natural, renewable and recyclable products and made from wood grown in sustainable forests. The logging and manufacturing processes are expected to conform to the environmental regulations of the country of origin.

P02123

# Contents

# Content Guidance

# Getting the most from this book

**Examiner tips**
Advice from the examiner on key points in the text to help you learn and recall unit content, avoid pitfalls, and polish your exam technique in order to boost your grade.

**Knowledge check**
Rapid-fire questions throughout the Content Guidance section to check your understanding.

**Knowledge check answers**

1 Turn to the back of the book for the Knowledge check answers.

**Content Guidance**

Exam-style questions

Examiner comments on the questions
Tips on what you need to do to gain full marks, indicated by the icon ⓔ.

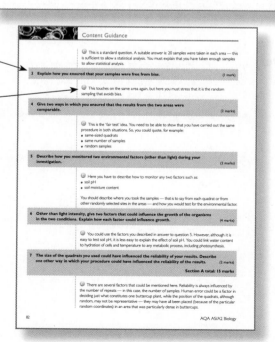

# About this book

This guide is written to help you to prepare for the Units 3 and 6 assessments of the AQA Biology specification introduced in 2008. These units aim to develop your investigative and practical skills. You are not required to learn a body of facts, rather to understand the principles of how to investigate a problem experimentally. These principles include how to:

- design the investigation
- carry out the investigation
- record and present the results from the investigation
- analyse the data obtained
- draw conclusions from the data using biological knowledge that allows interpretations to be made
- evaluate the reliability and validity of the investigation

**Examiner tip**
Don't forget that outlining the design of an investigation, analysing data, drawing conclusions from data and evaluating the reliability and validity of investigations could be tested by questions in the AS and A2 written tests.

This guide takes you through the stages of carrying out a biological investigation and shows you the aspects you should consider at each stage.

It examines the issues that are often raised in assessments and how to address these in your answers.

It is not possible to consider in detail some of the specific practical investigations used in assessments, although an indication of these is given. However, the principles used in all assessments are similar and these are addressed and illustrated with examples.

## How science works

This is a component in the biology specifications of all examination boards, including AQA. The aim is to help you understand the process of scientific work. The main aspects of 'How science works' (HSW) are described below.

- Scientists use pre-existing knowledge and understanding, theories and models to suggest explanations for phenomena.
- They design, carry out, analyse and evaluate scientific investigations to test new explanations.
- They share their findings with other scientists so that they may be validated, or not, as the case may be.

As a consequence of the work of scientists, there may be implications for society as a whole. You are expected to appreciate and make informed (not emotional) comment on such aspects as:

- the ethical implications of the way in which research is carried out
- the way in which society uses science to help in decision making

**Examiner tip**
Do practise making informed comments on social issues. However strongly you feel about an issue, answers such as, 'It is wrong to do this' or 'The scientists are playing at God' show no *biological* understanding and will not gain marks.

## How should I use this guide?

The guide lends itself to a number of uses throughout your course. You can use it:

- to help you design investigations
- to help you prepare your analysis
- to help you prepare your evaluation
- to help you understand the mechanics of HSW

# Preparing for the Unit 3 and Unit 6 assessments

## Terms used in assessments

You will be asked precise questions in the assessments. You can save time, and ensure you score as many marks as possible, by knowing what is expected. Terms most commonly used are explained below.

- **Describe** — this means exactly what it says — 'tell me about...' — and you should not need to explain why.
- **Explain** — give biological reasons for *why* or *how* something is happening.
- **Complete** — finish off a diagram, graph, flow chart or table.
- **Draw/plot** — construct some type of graph. For this, make sure that you:
  - choose a scale that makes good use of the graph paper (if a scale is not given) and does not leave all the plots tucked away in one corner
  - plot an appropriate type of graph — if both variables are continuous variables, then a line graph is usually the most appropriate; if one is a discrete variable, then a bar chart is appropriate
  - plot carefully using a sharp pencil and draw lines accurately using a ruler
- **From the**... — use only information in the diagram/graph/photograph or other forms of data.
- **Name** — give the name of a structure/molecule/organism etc.
- **Suggest** — i.e. 'give a plausible biological explanation for'; this term is often used when testing understanding of concepts in an unfamiliar context.
- **Compare** — give similarities *and* differences between...
- **Calculate** — add, subtract, multiply, divide (do some kind of sum) and show how you got your answer — *always* show your working.

# The process of science

## What is science?

The word science comes from the Latin word '**scientia**', which means 'knowledge'. Science is not just about *having* knowledge: it is a system of acquiring knowledge based on the scientific method. This is sometimes called **experimental science**, because it depends on experimentation to obtain information. Experimental science seeks to answer the question 'why?' It seeks to establish a **cause-and-effect** relationship between two factors.

One important idea in science is that any suggested explanation of a phenomenon should be *capable of being proved wrong*. If there is no way of proving it wrong, how can other people accept that it is correct? This is what distinguishes science from belief.

# What is the scientific method?

This is the process by which biologists and other scientists approach their work. For centuries, people based their explanations of what they saw around them on observations alone, without testing their ideas to see if they were true. One ancient belief was that simple living organisms could come into being by **spontaneous generation** — i.e. that non-living *objects* could give rise to living *organisms*. For example, every year in the spring, the River Nile flooded areas of Egypt, leaving behind mud containing nutrients that enabled the people to grow crops. Along with the muddy soil, large numbers of frogs appeared that were not around in drier times. From this observation, people concluded that muddy soil gives rise to frogs!

Similarly, before the invention of the refrigerator, animal carcasses were hung in butchers' shops that were always full of flies. So people believed that the meat had turned into flies!

# The main steps of the scientific method

The stages of the scientific method are summarised in Figure 1.

**Figure 1** The scientific method

So what happens at each stage? What is the biologist doing? The process is centred on producing and testing a hypothesis. What is meant by 'hypothesis'?

A hypothesis is an educated guess about a possible explanation. It has to be stated in such a way that a prediction from it can be tested by experiment. Let us use an example to illustrate the steps of the scientific method.

Observation: tomato seeds do not germinate inside tomatoes.

**Knowledge check 1**

You will have investigated the effect of temperature on the rate of an enzyme-controlled reaction. What prediction were you testing?

### Table 1

| Step of the method | What happens at this step |
|---|---|
| Ask a question | A biologist knows that tomato seeds germinate when they are planted. Why don't they germinate inside tomatoes? |
| Do background research | The biologist now checks scientific journals and the internet to see if this (or a similar) problem has already been investigated. The biologist finds out that plants contain growth regulators. |
| Construct a hypothesis and make a prediction from this hypothesis | 'There are chemicals in tomatoes that stop the seeds from growing while they are still inside the tomatoes.' This hypothesis is testable by an experiment. The biologist thinks that a chemical is responsible. How could we test that? We could try covering some seeds with tomato juice and others with water and see if any germinate. Based on the hypothesis, we can make a prediction: 'seeds covered in tomato juice will not germinate as well as seeds covered in water.' |
| Design and carry out an experiment to test the prediction | Put several tomatoes in a blender. Filter (strain) the blended material through some muslin. Collect the tomato seeds and wash them in distilled water. Place 20 seeds on filter paper in a Petri dish and cover them with the tomato juice obtained from filtering the tomatoes. Place another 20 seeds on filter paper in a Petri dish and cover them with the same volume of distilled water. Place the Petri dishes in a growth cabinet that will keep the temperature and lighting conditions constant. Leave the Petri dishes for 4 days. Check the number of seeds that have germinated in each condition. Repeat the experiment 50 times. |
| Analyse results and draw conclusions | Out of 1000 seeds sown in each condition, 668 germinated in the distilled water (13.36 per dish); 165 germinated in the tomato juice (3.3 per dish). Something in the tomato juice is affecting germination. The cells were filtered off, so it must be a chemical in the juice. |
| Accept or reject the hypothesis | The hypothesis is on the right lines; the tomato juice only contains chemicals, not cells, and it reduces germination. The hypothesis is accepted. However, in the tomatoes none of the seeds germinate. There is more work to do! |

| Step of the method | What happens at this step |
|---|---|
| Report results | The biologist must now decide whether or not to report the results to other biologists. Someone might take the work further and try to isolate the chemical responsible in order to determine what is stopping the seeds from germinating inside the tomatoes. |

# Disproving the idea of spontaneous generation

Remember the belief that rotting meat produces flies? In 1668, the Italian biologist Francesco Redi disproved this by using the scientific method.

Many scientists consider this to be the first true 'experiment'. Redi used wide-mouthed jars containing meat. He left some jars open to the air. Others he covered with a piece of gauze. After several days, maggots and then flies could be seen in the open jars; none appeared in the covered jars.

Redi had *hypothesised* that only flies could produce more flies and had *predicted* that, in his experiment, flies would be found only in the open jars, He maintained all the jars under the same conditions — he *controlled many variables*. This is crucial in a scientific investigation. If there are several differences between two experimental conditions, then any one of those differences *could* account for the outcome. However, if all the variables are controlled and the difference between the experimental groups limited to the factor under investigation, then any difference in results is likely to be due to this factor alone.

By choosing to cover some jars with gauze rather than an impermeable seal, Redi allowed air to enter all the jars, which controlled a variable that could have affected the outcome of the experiment. His results matched his prediction. When other people tried the experiment, they obtained the same results. Redi concluded that flies cannot be produced by rotting meat. He also went on to say that it is unlikely that any form of spontaneous generation is possible.

The invention of the microscope opened up the world of microbiology. Many people still believed that microorganisms could arise by spontaneous generation. It took the work of Louis Pasteur to disprove this. In 1859, Pasteur carried out experiments to show that the microorganisms that caused wine and broth to go cloudy came from the air and were not made from the wine/broth itself (Figure 2).

Pasteur boiled broths in swan-necked flasks to kill any microorganisms present. The boiling forced steam and air out of the flasks. When the boiling stopped and the broth cooled, air was sucked back into the flasks. Some contained a filter to prevent solid particles from getting into the growth medium from the air. Others had no filter, but in these, the dust (and the microorganisms) in the air settled in the lowest part of the neck of the flask. All the flasks were kept under the same conditions in his laboratory.

Pasteur found that the broths stayed clear for months. At the end of this time, he treated the flasks in one of three ways.
- He left some of them as they were.
- He broke the necks on some.
- He tilted others to allow the dust in the low part of the neck to mix with the broths.

**Knowledge check 2**

Redi controlled variables that could have affected the outcome of his experiment. Other than allowing air to enter the jars, name *two* variables he would have controlled.

The broths in the second and third groups of flasks turned cloudy (due to the presence of microorganisms) within days. The broths in the first group remained clear.

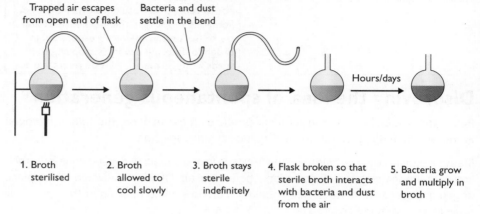

Trapped air escapes from open end of flask

Bacteria and dust settle in the bend

Hours/days

1. Broth sterilised

2. Broth allowed to cool slowly

3. Broth stays sterile indefinitely

4. Flask broken so that sterile broth interacts with bacteria and dust from the air

5. Bacteria grow and multiply in broth

**Figure 2** A summary of Pasteur's procedure

**Knowledge check 3**

Give *one* vital piece of information that Pasteur used to design his experiment.

After this, people were forced to admit that spontaneous generation, even of microorganisms, could not happen.

One stage in the scientific method is background research. Pasteur did this. He knew that other scientists had tried to disprove spontaneous generation and he drew on the results of their experiments and improved their technique.

# What do we mean by cause and effect?

Scientific experiments try to establish cause and effect. This means that they try to show that a change in one factor brings about a change in another factor. The factor that the scientist changes is called the **independent variable** (**IV**). The factor that the scientist measures to see if it changes when the IV is changed is called the **dependent variable** (**DV**). In the tomato seed investigation described earlier, the independent variable was the presence or absence of tomato juice. The dependent variable was the number of tomato seeds germinating.

**Examiner tip**

If it helps avoid confusion, remember '**I** change the **i**ndependent variable'.

To show that it *is* changes in the IV (and nothing else) that cause changes in the DV, we must take all possible steps to ensure that the experiment is a **fair test**. Other factors that could affect the results must be the same in all experimental conditions. Consider the tomato seed example. If one group of seeds had been at a higher temperature than the other group, this could have made the seeds germinate faster. We would not have known whether it was the tomato juice or the temperature affecting the results. The experiment would not be **valid**. Anything other than the IV that might influence the results must be kept constant. These are **controlled variables**. In the tomato seed investigation, the controlled variables included:

A **variable** is a factor that, if allowed to change, might affect the results of an experiment. A **controlled variable** is one that a scientist attempts to keep constant throughout an experiment.

- temperature
- lighting conditions
- number of seeds per dish
- volume of liquid (water or tomato juice) added

A **confounding variable** is a variable that you *can't* control and which might influence the results — it *confounds* the interpretation of the results. The presence of a confounding variable means that you cannot be certain that it is the IV that is producing the changes in the DV.

# Accuracy, precision, reliability and validity in scientific experiments

People often confuse these ideas. However, they are quite separate notions that are important in terms of how well an experiment is received by other scientists.

## Accuracy

If we could measure something with absolutely no errors, we would find its true value. Accuracy reflects how close our measurements are to their true value.

## Precision

Precision is an indication of the variation in repeated measurements of the same thing using the same instrument or procedure. If we make repeated measurements and our results show little variation, we can be confident that our results are precise.

The precision of our measurements is affected by the resolution of the instruments we use. The **resolution** refers to the smallest unit on the scale we are using to make measurements. The level of resolution chosen must reflect the magnitude of what is being measured. For example, to measure volume, you could use:

- a syringe
- a measuring cylinder
- a pipette
- a burette

To measure a volume of $2.5\,cm^3$ accurately, a $5\,cm^3$ graduated pipette has greater resolution, and would give repeated readings with greater precision than, say, a $250\,cm^3$ measuring cylinder.

To measure a large volume, say $200\,cm^3$, the resolution of a $5\,cm^3$ graduated pipette is probably not needed. Here, repeated measurements using a $250\,cm^3$ measuring cylinder would probably give adequate precision.

## Reliability

Reliability means 'Can we trust the results?' If, for example, other scientists repeat our investigation and get the same results, then our results are more likely to be considered reliable. There are several things we can do to increase reliability.

- Standardise the procedure. This makes it much more likely that we will be able to reproduce the results.
- Repeat the experiment many times. This should allow us to see a general pattern. It also allows us:
  - to spot odd results and, if justified, to exclude these
  - to calculate an average result, which is likely to be more representative than any individual result

**Examiner tip**

Examiners are unlikely to reward you simply for using the terms accuracy and precision; you must show that you understand what these terms mean. For example, you would gain marks for explaining clearly that you took five readings to find whether your measurements were very similar to each other, not simply for calling this precision.

**Examiner tip**

Really odd results are called anomalous results. If we are fairly sure that an error in technique caused the anomalous result, we are justified in excluding it when we analyse our data. If we have no idea what caused it, then the result must remain. We can't exclude it just because we don't like it.

- Try, wherever possible, to measure something rather than to use personal judgement. For example, if we have to wait until a solution turns a certain shade of red, one person's judgement will almost certainly differ from another person's. There are ways around this.
  - We can have a 'standard' with which to compare our experiment. In other words, something that is the exact colour needed. This helps, but we must still make a judgement.
  - We could use a **colorimeter**. This measures how much light passes through a liquid. It is nearly always better to *measure* than to *judge*.

## Validity

The evidence provided by an experiment is **valid** only if it answers the question being investigated.

There are two main types of **validity** that relate to scientific investigations:
- internal validity
- external validity

**Internal validity** is about whether or not an experiment measures what it says it is measuring. In the tomato seed experiment, the investigation claims to measure the effect of tomato juice on the germination of tomato seeds. We said that the difference in results from the two conditions was due to the presence or absence of tomato juice. For the experiment to be valid, we must be certain that the results were due *only* to the changes in the independent variable (presence or absence of tomato juice) and to nothing else. Had we not controlled all the other variables, the experiment would not have been valid.

**External validity** is concerned with whether or not the results of an experiment can be generalised to other situations. From the tomato seed experiment, can we conclude that chemical growth regulators prevent the germination of seeds in the fruits of, for example, different varieties of tomatoes or melons?

We would probably be fairly happy with the first idea, but may need a little more convincing about the second. It seems reasonable, but tomato plants and melon plants are very different, so we could be wrong. The external validity of our original investigation is limited.

**Knowledge check 4**

Scientists often use mice to test the safety of drugs intended for human use. Give *one* reason why this might be valid and *one* reason why this might not be valid.

However, if we had obtained similar results to the original investigation using the juice and seeds from apples, avocados, kiwi fruit and oranges, we would probably be happy to infer that this is also likely to be true for melons. We would have extended the investigation and could begin to see a pattern emerging that applies to all the fruits tested. We would, therefore, be more justified in concluding that it is likely to apply to all fruits. The external validity of our investigation has been increased.

# Content Guidance

# The Unit 3 assessment

## What you must be able to do

This unit addresses the following aspects of the AS subject criteria. The ability to:
- demonstrate and describe ethical, safe and skilful practical techniques, selecting appropriate qualitative and quantitative methods
- make, record and communicate reliable and valid observations and measurements with appropriate precision and accuracy
- analyse, interpret, explain and evaluate the methodology, results and impact of your own and others' experimental and investigative activities in a variety of ways

**3.3.1 Investigating biological problems involves changing a specific factor, the independent variable, and measuring the changes in the dependent variable that result.**

This means that you should be able to use your knowledge and understanding of the AS specification in order to:
- identify the independent variable and describe an appropriate method of varying it
- explain how you would choose values of the independent variable to collect a full range of useful quantitative data
- identify the dependent variable and describe how you would measure it
- describe and explain the level of accuracy to which you would measure the dependent variable
- identify other variables that might affect the results, and explain what the effect might be
- describe how these variables would be kept constant
- where necessary, describe how appropriate control experiments could be established, and explain why
- distinguish between accuracy and reliability and describe precautions needed to obtain valid, accurate and reliable data

**3.3.2 Implementing involves the ability to work methodically and safely, demonstrating competence in the required manipulative skills and efficiency in managing time. Raw data should be collected methodically and recorded during the course of the investigation.**

This means that you should be able to use your knowledge and understanding of the AS specification in order to:
- have due regard for the wellbeing of any living organisms that are part of an investigation, and also for the environment

**Knowledge check 5**

Would choosing temperatures of 0°C, 20°C, 40°C, 60°C and 80°C be appropriate in finding the optimum temperature of an enzyme? Explain your answer.

**Examiner tip**
Raw data are the results you collect during your investigation. Get into the habit of devising an appropriately labelled table in which to collect these data *before* you start any of the steps of the outline method.

**Examiner tip**
The specification states that you will *not* be asked to calculate standard deviation in a BIOL1 or BIOL2 unit test, but you might be asked to do it during Task 2 of BIOL3.

- carry out an investigation in a methodical and organised way, showing that you can:
  - use equipment competently and safely
  - manage your time effectively
  - make measurements to an appropriate level of accuracy and precision
- collect appropriate raw data and present these raw data in a suitable table

**3.3.3 Raw data may require processing. Processed data should be used to plot graphs that illustrate patterns and trends from which appropriate conclusions may be drawn. Scientific knowledge from the AS specification should be used to explain these conclusions.**

This means that you should be able to use your knowledge and understanding of the AS specification in order to:

- process raw data by carrying out appropriate calculations (such as calculating mean values and standard deviations)
- use the mean data to plot an appropriate graph (such as a line graph or bar chart, depending on the nature of the data)
- describe the trends and patterns in the data and, where appropriate, use specific values in the data to highlight significant changes
- recognise and distinguish between correlations and causal relationships
- draw valid conclusions, and use your biological knowledge and understanding to explain and justify these conclusions

**3.3.4 Limitations are inherent in the material and apparatus used, and procedures adopted. These limitations should be identified and methods of overcoming them suggested.**

This means that you should be able to use your knowledge and understanding of the AS specification in order to:

- identify aspects of the materials you use, the apparatus and your techniques and procedures that might affect the:
  - precision or reliability of your data
  - validity of your conclusions
- suggest *realistic* ways in which the effects of these limitations may be reduced

**Examiner tip**
If you are following the ISA route, your teacher will assess whether your practical techniques are safe and skilful during your laboratory sessions. Make sure you take these practicals seriously; 12% of the raw marks for your ISA are at stake!

# Unit 3 assessment: ISAs and EMPAs

There are two routes through which Unit 3 assessment can be delivered. Teachers at your centre will normally choose one of these routes for the whole centre. They are:

- **ISA (Investigative Skills Assessment)** Your teachers mark your practical assessments and submit the marks, and a selection of work as examples, to a moderator who checks the marking.
- **EMPA (Externally Marked Practical Assignment)** All the practical work you complete is marked by examiners; none of it is marked by your teachers.

Whichever route is chosen makes little difference to the nature of the tasks you have to undertake. The components of the two assessments and their approximate mark allocations are shown in Table 2.

### Table 2

| Assessment route | | | | | |
|---|---|---|---|---|---|
| **ISA** | | | **EMPA** | | |
| **Component** | **Marks** | | **Component** | **Marks** | |
| Practical skills assessment: your teacher submits an assessment based on your practical skills throughout the course. | 6 | | Practical skills verification: your teacher submits a verification of your practical skills, based on your work throughout the course. | 0 | |
| Task Stage 1: you carry out a task specified by AQA and record your results in a table you construct. You have to decide on some aspects of the task yourself (e.g. controls, volumes, number of repeats). | 4 | | Task 1: you carry out a task specified by AQA and record your results in a table supplied by AQA. You have to decide on some aspects of the task yourself (e.g. controls, volumes, number of repeats). You also answer some questions about aspects of the task. | 10 | |
| Task Stage 2: you process the data from stage 1 in an appropriate manner (e.g. calculate means, convert volumes of gas collected into rate of collection). | 6 | | Task 2: you carry out a second task specified by AQA and record the results in a table that you construct. You process the data in an appropriate manner and construct a graph. You answer questions on aspects of the investigation. | 10 | |
| Section A of written test: you answer questions based on the results from your own investigation. | 16 | | Section A of written test: you answer questions based on the results from your own investigation. | 15 | |
| Section B of written test: you answer questions based on related material supplied by AQA. | 18 | | Section B of written test: you answer questions based on related material supplied by AQA. | 15 | |
| Total for ISA | 50 | | Total for EMPA | 50 | |

At first glance, if your centre is following the EMPA route, you might think 'Hey, there are marks in the ISA for just doing things well all year long. I would be good at that and get 5 or 6 marks. Why aren't we doing the ISA?' You know that. Your teacher knows that. I know that and the AQA knows that. The marks for the ISA route of assessment are generally higher than those for the EMPA route. So guess what happens to the grade boundaries? Correct — the grade boundaries for the EMPA route are lower than those for the ISA route. If you want to check this for yourself, go to www.aqa.org.uk. Once on the home page, select 'Support', then 'Results statistics'. Select an examination session (e.g. June 2010), the type of examination (A-level) and scroll down until you come to the biology grades.

**Examiner tip**

Bear in mind that you will only find grade boundaries for the ISAs and EMPAs in the June series.

# The practical skills you will need

AQA assumes that you are familiar with the use of basic equipment, such as measuring cylinders, Bunsen burners, thermometers etc. You must be able to use the following equipment also.

## The use of water baths to change or control temperature

You can use a beaker of water heated to the temperature you need, but it will cool down. There are two solutions to this.

- You can use a Bunsen burner intermittently to heat the water to just above the desired temperature and then allow it to fall to just below the desired temperature. With practice, the temperature can be maintained to within ±2°C.
- You can heat the water to a few degrees above the desired temperature and accept that it will fall to just below the desired temperature over the course of the experiment. The 'average' temperature will, hopefully, be the desired temperature. This method is less satisfactory and can only be used when there is a large volume of water that will not cool down quickly.

Better still, you could use a thermostatically controlled water bath. This should keep the temperature more constant. But bear the following in mind:

- It does not keep the temperature completely constant. It does (automatically and more precisely) what you would do with a Bunsen burner and beaker of water.
- The temperature may not be exactly what the water bath says. You should check it regularly with a thermometer.

## The use of buffers to change or control pH

First, remember that pH measures the acidity or alkalinity of a solution. It measures the concentration of hydrogen ions relative to water. Solutions with a higher concentration of hydrogen ions than water have a lower pH and are acidic. Solutions with a lower concentration of hydrogen ions than water have a higher pH and are alkaline. The pH scale is shown in Figure 3.

**Examiner tip**

If asked how you would ensure you kept a water bath at a constant temperature, it is important you answer that during your investigation you measured the temperature with a thermometer several times. At the very least, answer that you measured the temperature at the start, at the end and once during your investigation.

**Figure 3** The pH scale

Adding just a tiny amount of a strong acid (or strong alkali) to a neutral solution changes its pH dramatically. Buffers are solutions that resist this change and help to maintain constant pH, within fairly narrow limits. Buffers can be prepared to maintain the pH of a solution at any given value.

**Examiner tip**

If asked how you would control pH as a variable, the answer is always to use a buffer solution.

# Producing an appropriate dilution series when provided with stock solutions of reagents

To test the effect of changing the concentration of a solution on the rate of a process or reaction, you have to prepare the different concentrations of the solutions. There are two ways of doing this.

- You can weigh out the appropriate amount of solid for each solution and dissolve it in distilled water.
- You can repeatedly dilute a stock solution until you produce the concentration needed. This is called **serial dilution**. In your Unit 3 assessments, the stock solution will be provided.

In a serial dilution, each solution along the series is less concentrated than the previous solution by a set factor. Often this factor is 10, but it need not be. Figure 4 shows how to dilute a solution by a factor of 10.

**Figure 4** A 10-fold dilution of a stock solution

**Knowledge check 6**

To what volume of water would you add I cm³ of stock solution to get an 8-fold dilution?

Notice that to get the 10-fold dilution factor, you add 1 cm³ of stock solution to 9 cm³ water, *not* to 10 cm³.

Sometimes dilutions are made with buffer solutions, so that the pH of each dilution is the same.

Figure 5 shows how to produce 2-fold, 5-fold and 10-fold serial dilutions of a stock solution using buffer solutions.

**Figure 5** How to produce a 2-fold, 5-fold and 10-fold dilution series of a stock solution by diluting with buffer solution

# Using an optical microscope, preparing temporary mounts, staining and estimating size

## Setting up and using an optical microscope

There is a clear sequence of steps to take to achieve perfect viewing.

1   Turn the nosepiece until the low-power objective lens is in position. (In changing from one objective to another, you will hear a click when the objective is set in the correct position.)
2   Turn on the substage light (or adjust the mirror if the microscope does not have one). Position the condenser as high as it will go and open the iris diaphragm using the lever beneath the condenser, which is below the stage of the microscope. This will give maximum light.
3   Using the coarse-focus knob, raise the objective lens away from the stage. Place a correctly prepared slide (see p. 20) on the stage and secure it with the stage clips (or mechanical stage depending upon which is present on your microscope). Place the slide with the object directly above the brightly illuminated sub-stage condenser.
4   Viewing the stage from the side, lower the low-power objective lens until the slide is almost (but not quite) touching it. Looking through the eyepiece, raise the objective lens slowly by turning the coarse-focus knob counter-clockwise until the object is in focus. Use the fine-focus knob to bring the object into sharp focus. If necessary, readjust the amount and intensity of light for comfortable viewing — sometimes a less intense light can give a better image.
5   To increase magnification, first, be sure your slide is focused under low power. Then, turn the nosepiece to the next highest powered objective lens. Watch from the side to make sure that the objective lens does not touch the slide. You may need to make a slight adjustment with the fine-focus knob to bring the object into sharp focus again.

(see p. 20)

**Figure 6** The main parts of a typical optical microscope

Eyepiece lens
Tube
Coarse focus
Fine focus
Revolving nosepiece of turret
Objective lenses
Stage with stage clips
Arm
Illuminator
Base

> ### Examiner tip
> Although it looks robust, the optics of an optical microscope are delicate. Always use both hands to carry an optical microscope; one holding the arm of the microscope and the other supporting its base.

> ### Examiner tip
> When looking through the eyepiece lens, always rack the objective lens upwards, *away* from the slide. This will ensure you do not damage the objective lens by smashing it into the glass slide.

## Preparing a temporary mount

To look at cells, or live specimens, you will normally prepare a wet-mount (temporary slide), as follows.

- Use a dropper pipette to place a drop of water on a clean slide.
- Put the specimen in the water drop.
- Lower one edge of the coverslip to the edge of the water drop as shown in Figure 7. Lower the coverslip slowly to avoid trapping air bubbles in the water, as these will interfere with viewing the specimen.

**Examiner tip**

Under the microscope, air bubbles appear as empty circles with a black outline.

**Examiner tip**

You will find it easier to lower a coverslip slowly, and avoid introducing air bubbles, if you hold the point of a mounted needle under the upper edge of the cover slip.

**Figure 7** Preparing a temporary mount

To stain a temporary mount:

- place a small drop of the stain you are using at one edge of the cover slip
- place a small piece of paper towel, filter paper or tissue paper in contact with the water *at the opposite edge* of the cover slip from the drop of stain (this will remove water from the slide, which will be replaced by the stain)

## The field of view and estimating the size of an object

When you view an object under the microscope it lies inside a circular field of view. If you know the diameter of the field of view you can estimate the size of an object seen in that field. Each different magnification has a different-sized field of view. As you increase the magnification, the field of view (and diameter) gets proportionately smaller.

### How to estimate the size of a cell

- Place your slide of cells (e.g. onion epidermis cells) under the microscope and get the cells in focus at magnification × 100.
- Keeping the magnification the same, remove the slide and replace it with a transparent plastic ruler.
- Focus on the millimetre scale on the ruler. You will probably see something like Figure 8.
- Use this to estimate the width of 'field of view'. You would probably estimate the field of view as shown in Figure 8 to be about 2 mm.
- Replace the slide of onion cells and re-focus.
- Count how many cells fit lengthways and widthways into the field of view.
- If eight cells fit across this field of view, the width of each cell is 2 mm ÷ 8 = 0.25 mm.

**Figure 8** Estimating the field of view

This is only one estimate. You should repeat the procedure in several areas of the slide and find the mean.

Remember to re-estimate the field of view if you change magnification.

# Collecting reliable quantitative data

## Data collection when a gas is evolved

'Evolution of gas' means the release of a gas. There are several ways in which a gas released by a reaction can be collected, and each has plus and minus points. One way is by displacing water from a container (Figure 9).

**Figure 9** One method of collecting a gas by displacing water

There are a several points to note.
- A burette is used to add the hydrogen peroxide. This has a tap so everything else can be set up and the hydrogen peroxide added last. None of the released gas will be lost.
- The graduations on a burette have high resolution, so an accurate amount can be added.
- The measuring cylinder is a graduated instrument, so the volume of gas released can be measured easily.

**Knowledge check 7**

Do the markings on a gas syringe give it high accuracy, high precision or high resolution? Explain your answer.

Another way is to use a gas syringe (Figure 10). The graduations on a gas syringe are usually $1\,cm^3$ apart, which allows you to estimate volumes to the nearest $0.5\,cm^3$. A burette is used to add the hydrogen peroxide so that none of the released gas escapes.

There are several variations on each method — for example a syringe might be used to add the liquid to the reaction vessel. In the first method, the gas could be collected in a burette for increased accuracy — but measuring cylinders are much cheaper!

Burette

Gas syringe

Conical flask

Catalase solution

**Figure 10** Using a gas syringe to collect a gas

The method chosen may be influenced by both the experiment and the number of repeats. For example, it is easier to disconnect, reset and re-use a gas syringe than it is to refill a burette or measuring cylinder with water and invert it, making sure that no water escapes.

## Data collection when a colour change takes place

There are several things that you might be asked to do in investigations involving colour changes, for example:

- describe the colour change that has taken place
- use the intensity of a colour change to estimate the strength of a solution
- measure how long it takes for a specified colour change to take place

**Examiner tip**

If you are colour-blind, you *must* let the examinations officer in your centre know so that s/he can make special arrangements with the examination board.

If you have to describe the colour that forms, you should have no problem, provided that you can remember the basic colours of the spectrum (and black):

red, orange, yellow, green, blue, indigo, violet (and black)

Try to stick with these and not invent others. Purple/mauve probably equates to indigo and/or violet. Remember that this is a science examination and no one is interested in artistic opinion.

If you have to time when a certain colour appears or disappears, you have to use personal judgement. The main problem here is knowing when a certain colour change has taken place, or how much of a colour change has taken place. People's opinion about the colour of a solution varies. To get consistent judgement of a colour change you must either:

- use a colour standard for comparison
- use equipment that can *measure* the colour of the solution (such as a colorimeter or a spectrophotometer)

## Using a colour standard

If you are asked to estimate the strength of a solution of glucose using the results from the Benedict's test, you will need colour standards (Figure 11) with which to compare the results.

To produce these, you would:

- make up solutions of glucose with a range of concentrations
- test each glucose solution with Benedict's solution and retain for reference

0%   1%   2%   3%   4%   5%   Unknown

**Figure 11** Colour standards for the Benedict's test using different concentrations of glucose solution

To ensure that these reference colours are a valid representation (that is, they do show what your labelling says they show) you must:

- use the same volumes of reagents each time
- heat to the same temperature each time
- heat for the same length of time each time
- stop the reaction immediately time is up by adding hydrochloric acid

Test the unknown solution in exactly the same way and compare its colour with the colour standards. It may match one of them or fall between two, either way you will be able to give an estimate of its concentration.

## Using a colorimeter

A colorimeter is a piece of equipment that measures the change in the intensity of light as it passes through a solution. Figure 12 shows what happens.

Incident light       Transmitted light       Detector

Light source       Sample

**Figure 12** How a colorimeter measures the change in intensity of light passing through a solution

When looking for a colour change, it is good practice to record when you think the change has occurred and then continue with the investigation to see if any further colour change occurs. If it does, you know your original judgement was wrong. If it does not, you know your original judgement was correct.

**Knowledge check 8**

Hydrochloric acid is used to stop the reaction between glucose and Benedict's solution. How does this ensure that the reference colours are a valid representation?

**Knowledge check 9**

In the example shown in Figure 11, what is the concentration of the 'unknown' glucose solution?

The colorimeter can record either:

- the percentage of light that passes through (percentage transmission) or
- the percentage of light that is absorbed (percentage absorbance)

The method is as follows.

- Make up standard solutions and test them with Benedict's solution.
- Place a small sample of each into a cuvette, place the cuvette in the colorimeter and measure the transmission or absorbance.
- Plot a graph of absorbance/transmission against concentration.

**Knowledge check 10**

In the example shown in Figure 13, what is the concentration of the 'unknown' glucose solution?

The graph is called a calibration curve or calibration graph. An example of a calibration curve using absorbance (more concentrated solutions are more intensely coloured and therefore absorb more light) is given in Figure 13. Knowing the absorbance of the unknown solution, its concentration can be read from the graph.

**Figure 13** A calibration curve

To measure how long it takes for a colour change to take place, you could use either colour standards or a colorimeter. In either case, you would take samples periodically and compare them with the colour standards or the calibration curve.

## Data collection when there are changes in mass or length

You measure changes in length using a ruler (or millimetre graph paper because it is easier) and changes in mass using a balance. All that is called for is care and patience. Make the measurements carefully and as accurately as the equipment will allow.

**Raw data** are the observations you record during your investigation. If you later use them to perform calculations, you produce processed data.

Get used to recording your **raw data** in a table as you go along. You should construct your table so that it shows all the repeats at all the conditions of the investigation. It should show the original condition, the new condition and the change in the condition. It need not show mean changes or percentage changes as these are processed data and not part of the experimental results.

For example, if you measured the change in mass of potato tissue in six different concentrations of sucrose solution and carried out three repeats at each concentration, your table would look something like Table 3.

AQA AS/A2 Biology

**Table 3**

| Concentration of sucrose/g dm$^{-3}$ | Repeat | Initial mass/g | Final mass/g | Change in mass/g |
|---|---|---|---|---|
| 0 | 1 | | | |
| | 2 | | | |
| | 3 | | | |
| 1 | 1 | | | |
| | 2 | | | |
| | 3 | | | |
| 2 | 1 | | | |
| | 2 | | | |
| | 3 | | | |
| 3 | 1 | | | |
| | 2 | | | |
| | 3 | | | |
| 4 | 1 | | | |
| | 2 | | | |
| | 3 | | | |
| 5 | 1 | | | |
| | 2 | | | |
| | 3 | | | |

**Examiner tip**
Always use the left-hand column of your table for the independent variable.

Increases in mass are shown as + (gain) and decreases as – (loss).

You need to be able to calculate both mean change in mass and percentage change in mass.

Mean change in mass is simple. For each concentration, add the changes, remembering to take note of the sign (some may be + and others –), and divide by the number of repeats. For this example:

$$\text{mean change} = \frac{(\text{change 1} + \text{change 2} + \text{change 3})}{3}$$

Percentage change is a little more complicated, but is quite easy once you understand the principles. You are converting the actual change to *a percentage of the original*. To do this you must:
• convert the actual change to a fraction of the original
• convert the fraction to a percentage

This is done in one simple calculation, as shown below.

$$\text{percentage change} = \frac{(\text{final} - \text{original}) \times 100}{\text{original}}$$

**Examiner tip**
You are likely to be asked to calculate a percentage change at least once in your series of AS Biology unit tests. Make sure you remember how to calculate them.

So, the percentage change in mass of a piece of potato that increased in mass from 2.6 g to 3.12 g is:

$$\% \text{ change} = \frac{(3.12 - 2.6) \times 100}{2.6} = \frac{0.52 \times 100}{2.6} = 20\%$$

The mass has increased, so the percentage change is positive. If the mass change had been a decrease of 0.52 g, the percentage change would be –20%.

# Specific investigations you need to know about

In addition to the practical skills described, there are certain investigations you need to know about. It is unlikely that you will be asked to carry out the particular version of these investigations that you have carried out in your school or college. However, you may be asked to carry out, and comment on, an investigation testing the same relationship in a different context.

For example, you might have carried out an investigation into the effect of pH on the activity of the enzyme catalase in decomposing hydrogen peroxide. You would have:

- devised a way of changing the IV (independent variable — pH)
- devised a way of measuring changes in the DV (dependent variable — rate of decomposition of hydrogen peroxide by catalase)
- controlled other key variables (such as temperature, enzyme concentration, substrate concentration, volumes of the enzyme and substrate solutions, time allowed for the reaction to proceed) in order to increase the internal validity of the experiment
- repeated the experiment a minimum of three times at each pH in order to increase the precision of the results
- recorded your results in a table
- calculated mean reaction rates for each pH value
- plotted a graph of mean reaction rate against pH
- analysed the graph and described any patterns
- explained the patterns using biological knowledge of enzyme action
- evaluated the experiment to highlight any unavoidable errors and other limitations that were a result of the equipment used or the procedure chosen and, if possible, suggested how these errors and limitations could be minimised

It is unlikely that an ISA would ask you to carry out a practical that is used widely in schools and colleges. The main reason for this is that there will be schools and colleges that do *not* use it and so their students would be at a disadvantage. You are more likely to be asked, for example, to carry out and comment on the effect of pH on an enzyme that you have not come across before. All the aspects described above will still apply, but you will have to work out, from the information given, how to measure the dependent variable.

In this investigation, you may have used apparatus like that shown in Figure 10 to collect and measure the volume of oxygen given off during the reaction.

**Knowledge check 11**

What could you measure to find the rate of decomposition of hydrogen peroxide in this investigation?

pH could be altered by adding different buffers to the catalase. Temperature could be investigated by standing the conical flask in a water bath at different temperatures. Using the same concentrations and volumes of catalase solution and hydrogen peroxide each time controls these variables.

In an ISA, you could be asked to investigate the effect of pH on any enzyme — for example pectinase. This enzyme increases fruit juice production by breaking down the pectin that holds cells together in fruits. You could use apples and investigate how much juice is produced at different pH values. You would use buffer solutions to vary the pH and control:
- the mass of apple tissue used (affects substrate concentration)
- the surface area of apple tissue
- temperature
- enzyme concentration
- volume of enzyme

You could follow this method.
- Chop apples of the same variety into 5 mm cubes.
- Weigh equal masses of chopped apple (50g) into separate beakers.
- Prepare enzyme solutions at different pH values by adding 1 cm$^3$ buffer solution to 19 cm$^3$ enzyme solution.
- Add 5 cm$^3$ enzyme solution to each beaker.
- Stir the chopped apple pieces to mix all the pieces with the enzyme.
- Put all the beakers into a water bath at 40°C for 20 minutes.
- Use paper coffee filters in funnels to filter the juice from the apple preparations into 100 cm$^3$ measuring cylinders (see Figure 14).

**Figure 14** Apparatus for filtering juice from apple preparations

Even though this experiment is very different from the catalase experiment, the same principles have been used. The pH has been changed by using buffers and the other key variables have been controlled.

When the context is completely new, the ISA task sheet will tell you how to carry out the basic investigation. It will tell you how to measure the dependent variable and give a good indication of how to change the independent variable. However, you will have to decide how to control any other variable(s) and also how many repeats you will need to carry out.

**Knowledge check 12**

In this investigation, it is important to control the surface area of the pieces of apple tissue. Explain why.

**Knowledge check 13**

Some of the apple preparation you would collect would be the enzyme in buffer solution you added. Would you subtract 5 cm$^3$ from the volume of preparation you measured? Explain your answer.

Table 4 lists the experiments prescribed by the specification. Any one of these may be used as the basis of an ISA. Remember, the context will almost certainly be completely new to you.

**Table 4**

| Practical | Independent variable | Dependent variable | Controlled variables |
|---|---|---|---|
| Effect of pH on enzyme activity | pH | Enzyme activity | Enzyme concentration, substrate concentration, reaction volumes, reaction time, temperature |
| Effect of temperature on enzyme activity | Temperature | Enzyme activity | Enzyme concentration, substrate concentration, reaction volumes, reaction time, pH |
| Effect of substrate concentration on enzyme activity | Substrate concentration | Enzyme activity | Enzyme concentration, pH, reaction volumes, reaction time, temperature |
| *The three investigations above are examples of the specification requirement that candidates should carry out investigations into 'the effect of a specific variable on the rate of reaction of an enzyme-controlled reaction'.* | | | |
| Effect of age on human heart rate | Age of individual | Resting heart rate | Exercise levels, gender, time of day, cigarette smoking |
| Effect of intensity of exercise on human heart rate | Intensity of exercise | Heart rate | Duration of exercise, type of exercise, age, gender, smoking |
| Effect of duration of exercise on human heart rate | Duration of exercise | Heart rate | Intensity of exercise, type of exercise, age, gender, smoking |
| *The three investigations above are examples of the specification requirement that candidates should carry out investigations into 'the effect of a specific variable on human heart rate or pulse rate'.* | | | |
| Effect of solute concentration on the rate of water uptake by plant tissue | Concentration of solution | Water uptake or loss by plant tissue | Duration of immersion of tissue, mass/volume of tissue, surface area of tissue, absence of surface water on tissue |
| Measurement of the rate of water uptake by means of a simple potometer | For example, wind speed | Rate of water uptake by a leafy shoot | Duration of practical, leaf area on shoot, air temperature, humidity |

| Practical | Independent variable | Dependent variable | Controlled variables |
|---|---|---|---|
| Collection and analysis of data relating to intraspecific variation | Different groups of organisms in the sample population, e.g. sex | Variable under investigation, e.g. height | Other variables in sample population, e.g. age |

*The last investigation in this table is unlike the others. The specification does not state any particular dependent variable in the sample population.*

# Other skills you will need

## Planning skills

### Distinguishing between the independent variable and dependent variable

The factor that a scientist (you, in this case) *changes* or *manipulates* is the independent variable (IV). The factor that is measured to see if it changes when the IV is changed is the dependent variable (DV). Table 5 identifies the IV and DV in some common investigations.

**Table 5**

| Investigation | IV | DV |
|---|---|---|
| The effect of pH on the activity of catalase | pH of mixture | Activity of catalase |
| The effect of concentration of solution on water uptake/loss by potato tissue | Concentration of solution | Extent of water uptake/loss |
| The effect of humidity on the rate of water uptake by willowherb shoots | Humidity of air | Rate of water uptake |
| The effect of cigarette smoking on resting heart rate | Number of cigarettes smoked per day | Resting heart rate |
| The effect of temperature on the rate of digestion of starch by amylase | Temperature | Rate of starch digestion |

Even if you do not know the experiment, the wording often gives it away, for example:

The effect of X .................................................................................................. on Y

(This is the one I'll change — the IV)       (This is the one I'll measure — the DV)

> **Examiner tip**
> If it helps you, remember **I** change the **i**ndependent variable.

## Operationalising variables

In the investigation into the effect of pH on the activity of catalase, pH is the IV and the activity of catalase is the DV. But how do you measure the activity of catalase? You have to restate the DV in a form in which it can be measured. This is called operationalising the variable.

How is this done? We need to look at what is happening during the reaction. Catalase is catalysing the breakdown of hydrogen peroxide ($H_2O_2$) into water and oxygen. We can summarise this in an equation:

$$2H_2O_2 \xrightarrow{\text{catalase}} 2H_2O + O_2$$

If catalase becomes more active, three things will happen:
- More hydrogen peroxide will be broken down (not easy to measure).
- More water will be formed (not easy to measure).
- More oxygen will be released (relatively easy to measure).

So, the rate of oxygen release can be used to measure the activity of catalase. As a result, the IV and DV become:
- IV — the pH (we can control and measure this)
- DV — the rate of oxygen release

Other examples of operationalising variables are shown in Table 6.

**Table 6**

| Unoperationalised variable | Operationalised variable |
|---|---|
| Rate of water uptake by willowherb shoot | Distance travelled by a bubble per unit time in a simple potometer |
| Extent of water uptake/loss by potato tissue | Increase or decrease in mass of potato tissue |
| Heart rate | Pulse rate |
| Amylase activity | Time taken for starch to be digested |

## Controlling key variables

In the introduction, we discussed the need for internal validity in investigations (in other words, we need to make them fair tests). To do this, we must change only one variable at a time; the others must remain as constant as possible. Table 7 lists the key variables that affect a number of biological processes. If you carry out an investigation into one of these, you must control all the others.

**Table 7**

| Biological process | Key variables | How controlled |
|---|---|---|
| Enzyme-controlled reactions | Temperature | Water bath |
| | pH | Buffer solutions |
| | Substrate concentration | Same concentration and volume of substrate solution for all repeats |
| | Enzyme concentration | Same concentration and volume of enzyme solution for all repeats |
| | Extent of reaction | Same time for all repeats |

| Transpiration | Temperature | Could use an environmental chamber to maintain or to vary this, but often difficult to control — monitor room temperature to see if it changes during investigation |
| --- | --- | --- |
| | Wind speed | Difficult to control, but can be varied using a fan |
| | Humidity | Enclosing plant in a bell jar or polythene bag creates a humid environment; placing silica gel (to absorb water vapour) in the container creates a dry environment |
| | Leaf area | Use plants with similar total leaf areas; express results as rate per $cm^2$ for comparability |
| Osmosis in plant tissue | Water potential of the plant tissue | Use the same source (e.g. the same potato) for all repeats; if this is not possible, make sure the different tissue is used evenly in all repeats |
| | Water potential of the external solution | Use the same concentration of external solution in all repeats |
| | Temperature | Water bath |
| | Surface area of tissue | Use tissue with the same dimensions and shape |
| Heart rate | Age | Make sure all participants are within same age range |
| | Smoking | The extent of smoking must be similar |
| | Exercise | Keep type and duration of exercise constant |
| | Gender | Use either male or female volunteers |
| Investigating the effect of environmental factors on intraspecific variation | Light intensity | It is not possible to control these, but they can be monitored using appropriate equipment. However, you must be careful not to take an unrepresentative reading. For example, an area in shade will give a low reading on the light meter; this may be different later in the day and you should take more than one reading to obtain an average and so give a more representative recording. |
| | Temperature | |
| | Soil pH | |
| | Soil water content | |
| | Wind speed | |

## Control groups

When investigating the effect of one variable on another, we need to know that it is the changes in the IV that are causing the changes in the DV. The usual way that scientists go about this is to set up a **control group** (also called a **control experiment**). If we want to be sure that the IV is causing the change in the DV, we should have a control group that is treated in the same way as all the other groups except for the value of the IV.

Let's go back to the catalase investigation in Figure 10.

We assume that it is the catalase in the conical flask that causes the breakdown of hydrogen peroxide and the release of oxygen. But we might be wrong — it could be happening spontaneously. A control flask in which distilled water replaces the catalase solution would settle the matter. The results from such an investigation are shown in Figure 15.

**Figure 15** Results of an experiment to investigate the effect of catalase on the breakdown of hydrogen peroxide

The control flask shows that there is a small amount of oxygen released spontaneously, but much less than in the experimental flask. Catalase is causing the difference. For each pair of measurements (see Figure 15), to find the true effect of the catalase we should subtract from the result of the experimental flask the volume of oxygen released in the control flask. If investigating the effect of temperature on the activity of catalase, ideally, we should set up a control flask at each temperature.

Some further examples of the use of control groups are shown in Table 8.

**Table 8**

| Investigation | IV investigated | Control group(s) |
| --- | --- | --- |
| Effect of substrate concentration on the activity of an enzyme | Concentration of substrate | Use distilled water instead of substrate solution |
| Effect of temperature on the rate of digestion of starch by amylase | Temperature | Use distilled water instead of amylase solution at each temperature |

---

A **control group** is treated in exactly the same way as the other groups in an experiment except for the value of the independent variable to which they are exposed. In some cases, this might mean exposing the control group to the absence of the independent variable.

**Knowledge check 16**

Describe what Figure 15 shows about the volume of oxygen released by (a) the experimental flask (with catalase) and (b) the control flask (with distilled water).

**Knowledge check 17**

Explain why the volume of oxygen released by the experimental flask levelled off in Figure 15.

| Effectiveness of different formulations of a drug | Drug formulation | Use placebo |
| Effect of intensity of exercise on heart rate | Intensity of exercise | Measure resting heart rate |
| Effect of wind speed on the rate of transpiration | Wind speed | Measure rate of transpiration in still air |

**Knowledge check 18**

In the first control group in Table 8, you would use distilled water rather than just add no enzyme. Explain why.

## Time management

In practical assessments, candidates often begin to carry out the tasks as soon as their teacher says that the assessment has started. They start to perform the first part of the investigation and sometime during or at the end of this they wonder how to go about the next stage. This is not a recipe for success. You need to spend some time at the start of the assessment organising your time.

The task sheet will tell you how to carry out the basic experiment. You must then decide:
- how to control the key variables
- how many repeats to carry out

You should think about the following questions.
- How long is each trial going to take?
- Will I have enough time to carry out repeats one after the other, or must I do them at the same time?
- If I do them at the same time, what must I do to make sure that I do not run some repeats for longer than others?
- Can I do anything to get the next set of repeats ready while the current set is running?
- What will I have to write down in my results table?

This last point is important, because it dictates the form that your table will take. There are two possibilities.
- Possibility 1: you will have to record a single figure for each trial (Table 9), such as the absorbance by a colorimeter, or the time taken for a certain colour to appear/disappear.

**Examiner tip**

Carrying out experimental tasks in an ISA or EMPA can be stressful. Spending a few minutes at the start to plan your time will reduce the stress later in the investigation.

**Table 9**

| Independent variable/units | Dependent variable/units | | | |
| | Repeat 1 | Repeat 2 | Repeat 3 | Mean |
| Condition 1 | | | | |
| Condition 2 | | | | |
| Condition 3 etc. | | | | |

**Examiner tip**

Although Table 9 has a column for 'mean', you do not have to include it in your table of raw data. The mean value is not a part of your raw data; it is part of your processed data.

- Possibility 2: you will have to record more than one figure per trial (Table 10) to get the actual figure you need — for example, to record by how much a sample of potato has changed length, you will have to record the initial length and the final length.

**Table 10**

| Independent variable/units | Repeat | Initial condition of DV/units | Final condition of DV/units | Change in condition of DV/units |
|---|---|---|---|---|
| Condition 1 | 1 | | | |
| | 2 | | | |
| | 3 | | | |
| Condition 2 | 1 | | | |
| | 2 | | | |
| | 3 | | | |
| Condition 3 etc. | 1 | | | |
| | 2 | | | |
| | 3 | | | |

**Examiner tip**
If your table headings do not fully describe the IV and DV, give this information in a title for the table.

Whichever form of table you use, make sure that you *construct it at the start of the investigation*. It does not matter that it is not the neatest table ever, but make sure that you keep to the following conventions:
- The headings must describe fully the condition you are changing/measuring.
- The different conditions for the IV should appear in the first column.
- The conditions for the DV should appear in subsequent columns.
- The units in which you measure the IV and the DV should appear in the column headings, *not* beside the figures in the body of the table.
- The body of the table should contain numbers only, not units.

# Analysing skills

You have obtained the raw data (your results), now you have to analyse them. The first step in this analysis is usually processing the data.

## Processing data

Why do we need to process the data? Surely, the results tell us what we want to know?

They probably do — but a research biologist may have to sift through pages of data and trends or patterns may not be apparent immediately. It can help us to see these trends if we can:
- reduce the number of figures we have to look at
- present the data in a way that shows the trends and also gives some idea of the variability of the data

**Examiner tip**
It is easier to see a trend in data in a graph than in a table. You can use this idea in a written test too. Sketch a rough graph of the data in the margin of the written paper, it may help you to see the trend.

### Mean and standard deviation

One way to reduce the number of figures we need to consider is to calculate the mean value for each set of data (for each set of repeats for a certain condition of the IV). Calculating the mean is quite straightforward:

$$\text{mean} = \frac{\text{sum of all the values for a set of repeats}}{\text{number of repeats in the set}}$$

Think back to the catalase experiment (catalase catalyses the breakdown of hydrogen peroxide into oxygen and water). The method of measuring the activity of the catalase is to collect the oxygen produced. Table 11 shows how long it took to collect a set volume (30 cm³) of oxygen at different temperatures.

**Table 11**

| Temperature/°C | Time taken to collect 30 cm³ oxygen/s | | |
| | Trial 1 | Trial 2 | Trial 3 |
|---|---|---|---|
| 10 | 54 | 47 | 43 |
| 20 | 12 | 14 | 16 |
| 30 | 5 | 5 | 5 |
| 35 | 9 | 5 | 4 |
| 40 | 9 | 6 | 9 |
| 45 | 14 | 11 | 11 |
| 50 | 73 | 71 | 57 |
| 55 | 119 | 109 | 132 |

If we look at the figures in Table 11, it seems fairly obvious that it takes considerably less time to collect 30 cm³ of oxygen at 30°C, 35°C and 40°C than at the other temperatures. It also seems clear that 35°C is the temperature at which the reaction occurs the fastest. However, the mean results (Table 12) show that there is little difference between the means for 30°C and 35°C.

**Table 12**

| Temperature/°C | Time taken to collect 30 cm³ oxygen/s | | | |
| | Trial 1 | Trial 2 | Trial 3 | Mean |
|---|---|---|---|---|
| 10 | 54 | 47 | 43 | 48.0 |
| 20 | 12 | 14 | 16 | 14.0 |
| 30 | 5 | 5 | 5 | 5.0 |
| 35 | 9 | 5 | 4 | 6.0 |
| 40 | 9 | 6 | 9 | 8.0 |
| 45 | 14 | 11 | 11 | 12.0 |
| 50 | 73 | 71 | 57 | 67.0 |
| 55 | 119 | 109 | 132 | 120.0 |

The mean shows the pattern in the results (Table 13).

**Table 13**

| Temperature/°C | Mean time to collect 30 cm³ oxygen/s |
|---|---|
| 10 | 48.0 |
| 20 | 14.0 |
| 30 | 5.0 |
| 35 | 6.0 |
| 40 | 8.0 |
| 45 | 12.0 |
| 50 | 67.0 |
| 55 | 120.0 |

**Knowledge check 19**

Would it be valid to conclude from Table 13 that the optimum temperature of the catalase was 30°C? Justify your answer.

You should, therefore, use the means (not raw data) to plot your graph.

Calculating the mean reduces the number of figures to be dealt with and shows overall trends more easily. However, calculating the mean can hide patterns in the data, particularly where more than one variable is at work. Look at Table 14, which gives some information about the oxygen consumption of chimpanzees walking on two legs and walking on four legs.

The means suggest that there is little difference in the oxygen consumption for the two styles of walking. However, we must be selective about using these mean values.

**Table 14**

| Individual tested | Oxygen intake/$cm^3 kg^{-1} min^{-1}$ | |
| --- | --- | --- |
| | Walking on two legs | Walking on four legs |
| Chimpanzee, 6-year-old male | 0.28 | 0.18 |
| Chimpanzee, 9-year-old male | 0.26 | 0.18 |
| Chimpanzee, 27-year-old male | 0.15 | 0.21 |
| Chimpanzee, 33-year-old female | 0.16 | 0.29 |
| Mean | 0.21 | 0.22 |

**Knowledge check 20**

We must be selective about using the mean values in Table 14. Use information in the table to explain why.

Some of the variability in the data is removed on calculating a mean — after all, that is the whole purpose of doing the calculation. However, we can show something of the variability of the data by calculating the standard deviation. This gives a spread within which 68% of values fall (34% above the mean and 34% below the mean). The reliability of the standard deviation increases with the number of data points included. With only three data points for each temperature in the catalase–hydrogen peroxide investigation, the standard deviation is less reliable than if we had carried out more repeats. Nonetheless, it can be calculated and it is included in Table 15. You are not required to know the formula for calculating standard deviation, merely to punch the raw data into your scientific calculator and press the 'SD' button to obtain the answer.

**Table 15**

| Temperature/°C | Mean time to collect 30 $cm^3$ oxygen/s | Standard deviation |
| --- | --- | --- |
| 10 | 48.0 | 7.2 |
| 20 | 14.0 | 2.0 |
| 30 | 5.0 | 0.0 |
| 35 | 6.0 | 2.6 |
| 40 | 8.0 | 1.7 |
| 45 | 12.0 | 1.7 |
| 50 | 67.0 | 8.7 |
| 55 | 120.0 | 11.5 |

This gives some idea of the variability of the data. But, does a bigger standard deviation mean more variability? Not always. If the numbers that make up the raw data are large, you would not be surprised if they were a little more variable than if they were smaller. So which is more variable, a mean of 67.0 with a standard deviation of 8.7 (at 50°C) or a mean of 48.0 with a standard deviation of 7.2 (at 10°C)?

One way of looking at this is to express the standard deviation as a percentage of the mean:

At 10°C: $\dfrac{(7.2 \times 100)}{48} = 15\%$         At 50°C: $\dfrac{(8.7 \times 100)}{67} = 12.3\%$

This suggests that even though the actual standard deviation at 50°C is bigger, it probably represents slightly less variability than the smaller standard deviation at 10°C.

Another way of assessing the variability of the data is to work out the **range**. This is the difference between the highest result and the lowest result in a data set. It is less useful than the standard deviation because:

- an extreme value at either end of the range will give a distorted picture of the variability of the data; such a value is termed an anomalous result
- the standard deviation uses every result obtained in its calculation, so is more representative

> The **range** is the difference between the smallest and largest value in a set of data. It is less representative of the variation in a set of data than the standard deviation, which uses all the values.

## Anomalous results

Look at the results in Table 16. They are from an investigation into the permeability of the cell surface membranes of beetroot cells at different temperatures. The amount of purple dye leaking out of the cells at each temperature is estimated by measuring the percentage of light that passes through (is transmitted through) a sample of water in which the beetroot tissue has been immersed for a set time. Are any of these results anomalous?

**Table 16**

| Temperature/°C | Colorimeter reading/% transmission | | | |
| --- | --- | --- | --- | --- |
| | Trial 1 | Trial 2 | Trial 3 | Mean |
| 0 | 100.0 | 98.5 | 99.0 | 99.2 |
| 22 | 93.9 | 95.0 | 96.0 | 95.0 |
| 42 | 80.1 | 77.0 | 76.9 | 78.0 |
| 63 | 26.3 | 29.9 | 31.0 | 29.1 |
| 81 | 0.7 | 0.9 | 1.1 | 0.9 |
| 94 | 0.0 | 0.2 | 0.2 | 0.1 |

There are two ways of spotting anomalous results:

- Results should be similar within a data set (all the results for a certain temperature should be similar). To check this, read across each row.
- Results should follow the overall trend (the trend here seems to be decreasing transmission with increasing temperature). To check this, look down the columns.

The set of results in Table 16 seems to conform to both these demands and we should have no hesitation in using all the results in each data set to calculate the mean.

Now look at the set of results in Table 17. Are any of these anomalous?

At first glance, it seems that most of the results in trial 3 (with the exceptions of those at 81°C and 94°C) are very different from those of the other two trials. But are they anomalous? They certainly affect the mean. The mean of all three results is shown first in the 'mean' column and the mean of just trials 1 and 2 is shown in brackets.

> **Knowledge check 21**
>
> Results should be similar within a data set. What feature of the results does this show?

**Table 17**

| Temperature/°C | Colorimeter reading/% transmission | | | |
| | Trial 1 | Trial 2 | Trial 3 | Mean |
|---|---|---|---|---|
| 0 | 100.0 | 98.5 | 84.1 | 94.2 (99.3) |
| 22 | 93.9 | 95.0 | 82.6 | 90.5 (94.5) |
| 42 | 80.1 | 77.0 | 69.3 | 75.5 (78.6) |
| 63 | 26.3 | 29.9 | 19.8 | 25.3 (28.1) |
| 81 | 0.7 | 0.9 | 0.4 | 0.7 (0.8) |
| 94 | 0.0 | 0.2 | 0.1 | 0.1 (0.1) |

However, the results from trial 3 show the same trend with temperature as those from the other two trials. Suppose we realise that we used tissue from a different beetroot for trial 3. We now know why the results are different from the other two trials. As the trend is consistent with the trends from trials 1 and 2, we are probably justified in including the results from trial 3 in the mean.

Look at Table 18. Are there any anomalous results and, if so, should we use them when calculating the means?

**Table 18**

| Temperature/°C | Colorimeter reading/% transmission | | | |
| | Trial 1 | Trial 2 | Trial 3 | Mean |
|---|---|---|---|---|
| 0 | 100.0 | 98.5 | 99.0 | 99.2 |
| 22 | 93.9 | 95.0 | 75.0 | 88.0 (94.5) |
| 42 | 80.1 | 77.0 | 76.9 | 78.0 |
| 63 | 46.3 | 29.9 | 31.0 | 35.7 (30.5) |
| 81 | 0.7 | 0.9 | 1.1 | 0.9 |
| 94 | 0.0 | 0.2 | 0.2 | 0.1 |

**Examiner tip**
Unless you can *explain* what looks like an anomalous result, you should include it when processing your data.

The two results highlighted are quite different from the other results in the data set. The anomaly at 22°C for trial 3 breaks the trend of temperature–transmission whereas that at 63°C for trial 1 does not. They both affect the mean, but not so much that the overall trend in the mean is disrupted.

So what should we do? Unless we can account for these anomalous results (possibly due to some fault in technique or equipment) we are stuck with them. We cannot discard them just because we don't like the look of them! We certainly cannot discard them just because they are the highest or lowest values in the data set. Suppose we had carried out five repeats at each temperature and for 22°C the colorimeter readings had been:

95.0   91.7   88.4   85.1   82.6

There is quite a difference between highest and lowest values and, on this basis, you might think that you should exclude these two values. However, the spread of the values is fairly even, so what justification is there for deciding that these two results are anomalous? Just being the highest and lowest is not sufficient reason. So you must include them, unless you decide that there is just too much variability and repeat all five trials.

## Drawing graphs and charts

Graphs are pictorial ways of representing data so that trends become more apparent. The type of graph (or chart) drawn depends on the type of data. To obtain results in biological investigations we usually measure or count something. We record such things as:

- how fast?
- how many?
- how much transmission?
- what volume?

Therefore, we end up with a number for the DV in each repeat of each condition of the investigation. What really determines the type of graph drawn is the nature of the IV. The IV could be either:

- **discontinuous** or categoric — there are two or more separate conditions for the IV and results are recorded for the DV in each of these separate conditions
- **continuous** — there are several conditions of the IV that form part of a continuous range of possible conditions (for example, five different temperatures between 20°C and 70°C are a sample of a continuous range of temperatures)

There are three main types of graph that you will draw in AS biology:

- **line graphs** — plotted between two continuous variables when there is likely to be a causal link between the IV and the DV
- **bar charts** — plotted when the IV is discontinuous (categoric) and the DV is continuously variable
- **scattergrams** — plotted when both variables are continuous but a causal link cannot be assumed (usually due to lack of control of other variables)

This is summarised in Table 19.

**Knowledge check 22**

You investigate whether students in your year group are right-handed or left-handed. What type of graph should you use to represent these data? Explain your answer.

**Table 19**

| Investigation | IV data type | DV data type | Type of graph |
|---|---|---|---|
| Effect of temperature on release of oxygen from hydrogen peroxide by catalase | Continuous (temperature) | Continuous (volume of oxygen) | Line graph |
| Frequency of blood group A in age groups 15–20 and 35–40 | Discontinuous (two separate ages) | Continuous (a frequency) | Bar chart |
| Effect of soil pH on the percentage of clover leaves with white V shapes | Continuous (pH value) | Continuous (percentage of clover) | Scattergram (since we cannot control other variables in a field) |
| Effect of water potential of surrounding solution on water gain/loss in potato tissue | Continuous (water potential of solution) | Continuous (change in mass) | Line graph (note, might have to show + and −) |
| Effect of intensity of exercise on heart rate | Continuous (intensity of exercise) | Continuous (heart rate) | Line graph |

You should always plot the independent variable on the *x*-axis of the graph and the dependent variable on the *y*-axis.

Mean values, when calculated, are used in plotting graphs. It might also be helpful to calculate the standard deviation of each mean and to show this on the graph to give some idea of the variability (and therefore precision) of the data. Figure 16 is a **scattergram** showing how the temperature of the surface of the eyeball and the temperature inside the rectum change as the external temperature changes.

**Knowledge check 23**

The data in Figure 16 are shown as a scattergram. Explain why.

**Figure 16**

Notice that:

- the temperature of the eyeball changes more than that of the rectum as the air temperature changes — this is shown by the different gradients of the two sets of data
- the temperature of the surface of the eyeball is generally more variable than that of the rectum — this is shown by the larger bars for the standard deviation
- the temperature of the eyeball is less than that of the rectum, except at 35°C, when the standard deviations overlap

If the standard deviation bars do not overlap (they don't for the other air temperatures) then, statistically, we can be confident that the two plots represent different values. However, when the standard deviation bars do overlap (as they do at 35°C) then, statistically, we cannot be confident that the two plots represent different values.

At AS, you are not expected to be able to explain this in terms of probability. You just need to know that overlapping standard deviations prevent us from being confident that two mean values represent truly different things.

Notice also that the points in Figure 16 are not joined. This is because the graph shows the relationship between two naturally occurring variables. Other variables are not controlled, so we cannot attribute cause and effect to the situation and so we do not connect the plots. They are left as a scattergram.

**Examiner tip**

If the standard deviation bars of two means overlap, the difference between the means is probably due to chance.

Figure 17 is a **bar chart**. The independent variable is discontinuous — four species of tree.

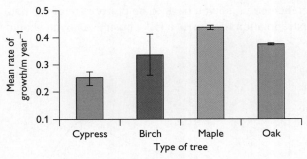

**Figure 17**

The dependent variable (mean rate of growth) is continuous, so we can show bars for the standard deviations as well as plotting bars for the actual rates. By comparing pairs of trees you can work out whether the growth rates are truly different or not.

Figure 18 is a **line graph**. It shows the effect of pH on the activity of urease, an enzyme that catalyses the conversion of urea into ammonia.

Note that in this graph, the plots are joined by ruled lines. A smooth 'curve of best fit' is not drawn. There is no hard-and-fast mathematical rule about when to draw a curve of best fit, and when to join plots with ruled lines. However, in this instance there are several gaps in the data. There are no results between pH4.5 and pH5.0. When intervening values (values between two plots) are uncertain, we should join the plotted points with ruled lines. If we had both those results and some others (such as values for pH3.7, pH5.8 and pH6.2) we could be more certain that all the plots are likely to be on a curve and we could draw a curve of best fit. The more data points there are, the more likely you are to be justified in drawing a curve of best fit.

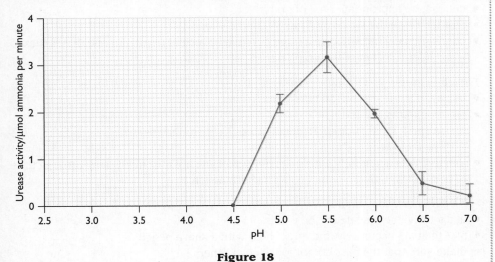

**Figure 18**

Being able to take a reading from a point on a line joining two plots is called **interpolation**. This is one of the values of a graph. Interpolation allows estimation of the DV at levels of the IV that have not been tested. **Extrapolation**, however, is a

**Knowledge check 24**

Is the difference in the mean growth rate of cypress trees and birch trees shown in Figure 17 due to chance? Explain your answer.

**Examiner tip**

If in doubt, always join plotted points with straight lines. You will never 'lose' marks for doing this, whereas you might for drawing an inappropriate curve of best fit.

**Examiner tip**

It is a convention that we refer to any line on a graph as a curve — even if it is a straight line.

different matter. Extrapolation means extending the curve (which might be a straight line) of a graph assuming no change from the last known slope of the curve. There is no other reference point, so you have to be pretty sure of the data to extrapolate. In particular, 'extrapolation to zero' is a risky business — you should be careful with this.

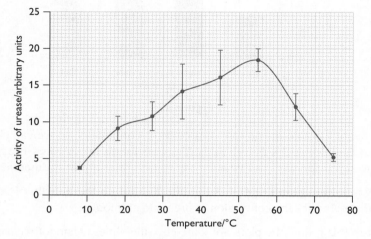

**Figure 19**

**Examiner tip**

In your ISA or EMPA, you are likely to be penalised if you extrapolate your graph to zero. Your best course of action is *not* to do it.

Look at Figure 19, which shows the effect of temperature on the activity of urease. For completeness, the x-axis shows 0°C, but the lowest temperature used in the investigation was 8°C. The curve has not been extended to zero because we do not know what the activity of urease would be at that temperature; we cannot assume it would be zero arbitrary units.

When you are plotting graphs, make sure that you:
- choose the appropriate type of graph
- plot the IV on the x-axis and the DV on the y-axis
- choose scales that will give a large curve, with a clear trend, not one that is tucked away in one corner of the graph paper

For a line graph, you should:
- use a truly linear scale on both axes
- plot the points accurately:
  - use small crosses or small dots with a circle around them
  - draw them with a sharp pencil
- join the plots accurately with ruled lines or, if you are absolutely sure, draw a curve of best fit through the points using a sharp pencil

For a bar chart, you should:
- use a truly linear scale on the y-axis
- plot the bars accurately and draw them with a sharp pencil
- make sure that the bars do not touch each other

## What do we mean by a 'truly linear scale'?

Look carefully at the *x*-axis of the urease graph in Figure 18. The pH values are spread evenly along the *x*-axis. A certain distance along the *x*-axis always corresponds to the same change in pH. This is a linear scale. Now look at the version of the graph in Figure 20.

**Figure 20**

In this graph there are two things to note about the scale on the *x*-axis.

- It is not linear — the same distance can represent different changes in pH, for example:
  - the first 'unit' of distance corresponds to a change in pH from 0 to 1.5
  - the next two 'units' correspond to a change in pH of 0.5
- The scale chosen results in a lot of wasted space on the graph; you do not have to start graphs at 0,0. The *x*-axis could have been started at 2.5, 3.0 or even 3.5, giving more space to plot the graph and make the trend clearer.

## Interpreting and explaining data

Once graphs or bar charts have been drawn, we are better placed to describe any trends or patterns in the data. This should be done accurately and fully. We might then be asked to use biological knowledge to try to explain these trends. Figure 21 shows the effect of substrate concentration on enzyme activity.

What is the best way to describe the trends shown in Figure 21? In describing a trend, we do not re-state every result — they should be recorded in the results table. However, it can be useful to quote one or two figures to help the description, for example:

- As the substrate concentration increases from 0 to 0.02 arbitrary units (a.u.), the rate of enzyme activity increases rapidly.
- From 0.02 a.u. to 0.1 a.u., the rate of enzyme activity still increases quite quickly, but the rate of increase is slowing.
- From 0.1 to 0.5 a.u., the enzyme activity increases only slightly; it is almost constant.

**Examiner tip**

When describing a graph, write about the overall trend, using figures from the axes to describe where the gradient of the curve changes. Do *not* describe each plotted point.

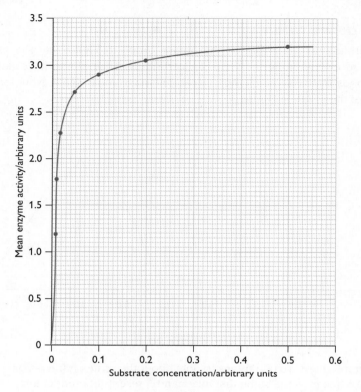

**Figure 21**

**Knowledge check 25**

When describing the graph in Figure 21, many students might write 'Above a substrate concentration of 0.1 arbitrary units, enzyme activity slows down'. This answer would not gain marks. Explain why.

**Examiner tip**

When asked to explain you must give *reasons* in your answer.

Having established the trend, we can use our biological knowledge of enzyme activity to explain it:

- If there is no substrate there can be no enzyme–substrate complexes (ES complexes) formed and so the enzyme activity will be zero.
- As the substrate concentration increases, more and more ES complexes are formed per second and so the enzyme activity increases.
- When the substrate concentration is so high that all the active sites are occupied at any given moment, the reaction cannot proceed any faster and the enzyme activity remains constant at its maximum rate for these conditions.

This explanation takes account of all the changes in activity that are evident in the graph and explains them in a way that is reasonable to expect from an AS biology student. The following are important when explaining the trends in results:

- Make sure you have the trends clearly in your mind.
- Think clearly about what is happening when the DV changes. You may have to 'unoperationalise' the DV to do this — for example, increasing amounts of oxygen being collected (per unit of time) as catalase catalyses the breakdown of hydrogen peroxide translate into increasing activity of catalase.
- Try to think why a change in the IV should change the unoperationalised DV.

When drawing conclusions be careful not to suggest a causal relationship when one has not been established. Data relating to intraspecific variation often show a correlation between two variables but, because other variables are not controlled, cause and effect is not established. Consider the data in Table 20 about leaves from nettle plants growing in the light and others growing in the shade.

**Table 20**

| Condition | Surface area/cm$^3$ | |
|---|---|---|
| | **Total of 30 leaves** | **Mean** |
| Light | 680 | 22.67 |
| Shade | 796 | 26.53 |

There seems to be a negative correlation between light intensity and surface area of nettle leaves. However, there are other uncontrolled factors, so we are not justified in saying that change in light intensity causes a change in leaf size. We must just report the negative correlation and leave it there.

# Evaluating investigations

When scientists report their investigations to other scientists (usually in scientific journals), they have to make clear the limitations of their investigations. They should include an evaluation of:

- the limitations of their equipment
- the limitations of their procedures
- the reliability of their results
- the validity of their conclusions

## Evaluating equipment

When you come to evaluate the equipment you are using, think about the following. We can use the collection of oxygen from the breakdown of hydrogen peroxide by catalase as an example (see Figure 10, page 22).

Ask yourself the following questions.

**(1)** What is the equipment supposed to do in my investigation *if it works perfectly*?
Answer: 'if it works perfectly' is an important caveat. If the gas syringe connected to the reaction vessel in Figure 10 works perfectly, it will collect all the oxygen released by the reaction.

**(2)** How might it not be working perfectly?
Answer: there might be leaks or delays that would result in some of the oxygen escaping.

**(3)** What impact might this have on my results?
Answer: this would result in all the readings being lower than they should be.

Bear in mind that graduated (measuring) equipment is not perfect. As a rough guide, whatever the graduations are, there could be an error of half of one of these graduations. For example, if you measure 5 cm$^3$ in a syringe marked in 1 cm$^3$ graduations, the volume could be anything between 4.5 cm$^3$ and 5.5 cm$^3$. As a percentage of the volume being measured, this is quite an error. 0.5 cm$^3$ as a percentage of 5 cm$^3$ is 10%. So, there could be a built-in error of 10% in all your results, simply because of the equipment you chose to use.

There are two solutions to this particular situation:

- Use equipment capable of greater resolution (e.g. a syringe or pipette with 0.1 cm$^3$ graduations).
- Use larger volumes — a 0.5 cm$^3$ error as a percentage of 20 cm$^3$ (rather than 5 cm$^3$) is an error of only 2.5% (rather than 10%).

**Knowledge check 26**

Suggest *two* uncontrolled variables that might affect the results in Table 20.

**Knowledge check 27**

Name the equipment you would use to measure a volume of 200 cm$^3$. Justify your answer.

You may be able to calculate the percentage error for several different pieces of equipment used in the investigation. Do not try to give an overall percentage error by adding these together. A simple addition is not appropriate — the overall assessment is much more complicated. We cannot go into the maths of this here, so trust me. Report the individual percentage errors and leave it at that!

## Evaluating procedures

When evaluating procedures, you should use a similar logic to evaluating equipment. Again, we can use the catalase investigation as an example. You should ask yourself the following questions.

**(1)** What is the purpose of each procedure, if I carry it out perfectly?

Answer: in the catalase investigation, using a stopwatch allows you accurately to find how long it takes to collect a certain volume of oxygen; you must start the stopwatch as soon as the hydrogen peroxide is added to the catalase.

**(2)** Why might I not be able to carry it out perfectly?

Answer: turning the tap on the burette and starting the stopwatch as soon as you swirl the flask to mix the hydrogen peroxide with the catalase may not be physically possible. You will also have to judge when the volume in the gas cylinder has reached (say) 30 cm$^3$.

**(3)** How might this affect my results?

Answer: depending on how you choose to solve the problems above (and you must be consistent in this — it must be a standardised procedure), you could record a time that is too short (if you start the stopwatch fractionally after the mixing has started), or too long (if you start the stopwatch and then turn the burette tap).

## Evaluating data

There are several questions you can ask that influence the reliability of the data. They vary slightly according to the type of investigation. Points to consider for laboratory investigations are shown in Table 21 and points to consider for ecological investigations (in your A2 coursework) are shown in Table 22.

**Table 21**

| Point to consider | Possible consequences |
|---|---|
| Did I use enough data points across the range (e.g. did I investigate enough temperatures)? | Too few means that the individual data points will be more widely spread and interpolation (assuming the trend between two points) will be less reliable. |
| Were the data points appropriately spaced (e.g. did I space the temperatures every 10°C)? | Inappropriate spacing of the data points affects interpolation. Where there are wide gaps, interpolation of data is much less reliable. For example, widely spaced temperatures will not allow you to find the optimum temperature of an enzyme accurately. |
| What do the standard deviations show? | If you have calculated standard deviations, then large values (as a proportion of the mean) indicate a lot of variability in your data — they are less reliable than data with smaller standard deviations. |
| Did I carry out enough repeats? | With too few repeats, the mean will be unduly affected by anomalous data; the risk of the data being unrepresentative is increased. |

| | |
|---|---|
| Did I measure to an appropriate degree of accuracy? | If the measurements were less accurate than they could have been, there will be a larger percentage error in the data, decreasing the precision of the data. |
| Did I have to use personal judgement at any point? | This is sometimes unavoidable (e.g. if you have to judge when a colour is formed or disappears). It is a limitation and *will* introduce a degree of variability in your data. Include in your evaluation any steps you took to minimise the effect (e.g. using colour standards). |
| Did I standardise all my procedures? | Even if you did, there may still be an error in your results. (If, in the catalase investigation, you start the stopwatch fractionally after the mixing has started, you will record a time that is too short.) This is a **systematic error** — it will affect all results in a similar way and you can allow for this. Varying the procedures introduces *unsystematic* errors that you cannot allow for and which make your results less reliable. |
| Did I control all the variables I could have controlled? | This is more likely to affect the validity of the investigation than the reliability. You may still produce repeatable (precise) results, but, if you did not control (say) the pH, then the results will not be a measure of what you intended, so they will not be valid. |

**Table 22** Points to consider when carrying out ecological investigation (A2 coursework)

| Point to consider | Possible consequences |
|---|---|
| Was the overall sample size large enough (Did I take enough readings?) | A small sample is less likely to be representative of the population as a whole and will be more easily affected by anomalous data. |
| For an investigation into numbers in an area:<br>• Were the sample points randomly allocated?<br>• Were there sufficient sampling points? | • Non-random allocation of the sampling points introduces bias into the investigation. Bias reduces both reliability and validity because some areas/individuals are more likely to be included than others.<br>• Too few points means anomalous results will have a large effect on the mean and, therefore, on the estimate of overall numbers. |
| For an investigation into distribution across an area:<br>• Were the sampling points allocated systematically (e.g. every 10 metres)?<br>• Were there sufficient sampling points? | • Systematic allocation of sampling points (systematic sampling) is the best way to observe changes in abundance across an area; random allocation of sampling points could miss a key section (see Figure 22).<br>• Too few points means that some species and some changes in abundance could be missed. |
| What do the standard deviations suggest? | Large standard deviations (as a proportion of the mean) suggest considerable variability in the data and, therefore, less reliability. |
| Did I control the variables that could be controlled? | If you measured the light intensity of two areas that could be in sunlight or shade at different times of the day, did you measure them both in sunlight (or shade)? Failing to do this will introduce serious non-systematic errors and reduce the validity of your conclusions. |

| Did I monitor the main variables that I could not control? | It is impossible to control all the variables in the field. However, several factors might (and probably will) vary between the sampling points. You should monitor as many of these as possible so that you can take into account the possible impact of changes in these variables when drawing your conclusions. Not monitoring key variables means that there could be effects of which you are unaware and this would reduce the validity of your conclusions. |
| --- | --- |

**Figure 22** Systematic and random sampling along a transect

# What might a Unit 3 ISA (or EMPA) task look like?

## AS Biology ISA (EMPA) Biol3 Task Sheet

*The effect of substrate concentration on the activity of an enzyme*

### Introduction

Catalase is an important enzyme in living cells as it breaks down hydrogen peroxide into water and oxygen. In this task you will investigate the changes in the volume of oxygen given off when catalase is mixed with hydrogen peroxide solutions of different concentrations.

### Outline method

You are provided with:
- five hydrogen peroxide solutions, each with a different concentration
- catalase solution
- conical flask with side arm
- bent glass tubing with attached rubber tubing
- burette/rubber bung assembly for the conical flask
- stand, boss and clamp to hold the burette
- trough
- $100\,cm^3$ measuring cylinder
- stopwatch
- $20\,cm^3$ syringes

You may ask your teacher for any other apparatus you require.
1  Place 20 cm³ of the least concentrated solution of hydrogen peroxide in the burette.
2  Place 20 cm³ of catalase solution into the conical flask
3  Assemble the apparatus as shown in Figure 23. Make sure the measuring cylinder is full of water.

**Figure 23**

4  Add the hydrogen peroxide solution to the catalase. Immediately, start a stopwatch.
5  Record data that will allow you to find the rate of enzyme activity
6  Repeat steps 1–5 for all the concentrations of hydrogen peroxide.

You will need to decide for yourself:
- what data to collect in order to allow you to calculate a rate of enzyme activity
- how many repeats to use with each concentration of hydrogen peroxide
- how to control variables that might influence the data to be collected

Use the space below to process your data.

Use the graph paper to plot a graph of your processed data.

Hand in this sheet at the end of the practical session.

You have to:
- carry out the investigation
- record your results in a suitable table
- process your data and plot a suitable graph

# Carry out the investigation

The basic instructions are given. In order to calculate a rate of enzyme activity, you must measure both the volume of oxygen collected and the time taken. You must keep one of these constant (a controlled variable) for each repeat — it does not matter which. The person marking your work will be able to tell from your table whether or not you have done this.

You need to control appropriate variables. Table 4 states that enzyme-controlled reactions are influenced by:

- temperature
- pH
- enzyme concentration
- substrate concentration
- extent (time) of reaction

Here, you are investigating substrate concentration, so you should try to control the other variables. You will probably be asked about this in the ISA (or EMPA) written paper.

## Record your results in a suitable table

Remember that the layout of a table should have the IV in the first column and results for repeats of the DV in other columns; units should be in the heading and not in the body of the table. You could use a table similar to Table 23.

Notice that a column for 'mean' is included in Table 23. You will not need this initially, as the mean is part of your processed data. However, you will need it when you come to work out rates ready to plot your graph. Notice also that the heading for the DV results takes account of both the volume of oxygen collected and the time taken — in this case, how much oxygen is collected in a set time (time is a controlled variable).

**Table 23**

| Concentration of hydrogen peroxide/% | Volume of oxygen collected in 60 seconds/$cm^3$ | | | |
|---|---|---|---|---|
| | Repeat 1 | Repeat 2 | Repeat 3 | Mean |
| Concentration 1 | | | | |
| Concentration 2 | | | | |
| Concentration 3 | | | | |
| Concentration 4 | | | | |
| Concentration 5 | | | | |

## Process your data and plot a suitable graph

Your must always plot the IV on the *x*-axis against the DV on the *y*-axis. In this investigation:

- IV is the concentration of hydrogen peroxide
- DV is the rate of the catalase-controlled reaction

To present data as rates, they must be in the form of 'something per unit of time' — for example, miles per hour or kilometres per second are both rates of movement. Here, it is 'volume of oxygen given off per second' (or per minute if you prefer). To get the data in this form, you need to:

- calculate the mean for each concentration
- divide this mean by 60 to give a mean volume per second

You can now plot your graph. An example is given in Figure 24.

**Figure 24**

# The written test

In Section A of the ISA (or EMPA) written test, you have to answer questions about your investigation, or results based on a similar investigation.

## Section A

These questions are about your investigation on the effect of substrate concentration on the activity of an enzyme.

You should use the task sheet, your results and any calculations you have carried out to answer these questions.

Answer *all* questions in the spaces provided.

| **I** **What was the independent variable in your investigation?** | (I mark) |

ⓔ The concentration of hydrogen peroxide.

| **2** **Describe how you controlled two other variables in your investigation.** | (2 marks) |

ⓔ You could describe techniques such as the use of a buffer to control pH and a water bath to control temperature.

| **3** **You were told to make sure that the measuring cylinder was full of water. Explain the importance of this.** | (2 marks) |

ⓔ If there had been any air in the measuring cylinder, the measurements of the volume of oxygen could be inaccurate. It is important to go on to say that this would influence the reliability of the results or that you took an initial reading of the air in the cylinder and subtracted this from your final reading.

| **4** **Explain two benefits of carrying out repeat investigations.** | (3 marks) |

e The main benefits are that repeats allow the identification of anomalous results and make it possible to take an average value, which is likely to be more representative than any single value.

**5  A student carried out a similar investigation to you. Figure 25 shows how this student plotted her results.**

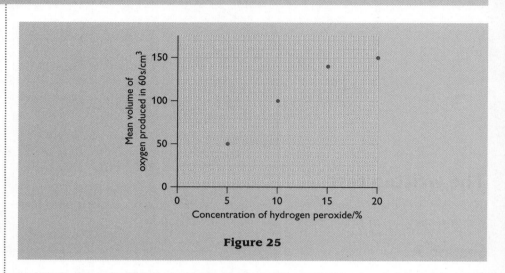

**Figure 25**

**Examiner tip**

Examiners provide a second graph like this to make sure that everyone has the same data. You might have made mistakes in your own investigation and examiners do not want these mistakes to be carried forward to the next stage of the ISA or EMPA.

**(a) Use the points to plot a curve.**                                                    (2 marks)

**Knowledge check 29**

How would you join the points in Figure 25? Explain your answer.

e It is important to remember that you can either:
- join all the plots with ruled lines, *or*
- where there is a clear trend, draw a curve of best fit

Remember that there are no data for 0%, so you must not extrapolate your curve to zero.

**(b) Use your curve to find the volume of oxygen produced when the concentration of hydrogen peroxide solution was 7%.**                                       (1 mark)

e In this situation, the examiner will try not to 'carry forward an error'. If you have made an error in drawing the curve, but read information correctly from your 'wrong curve', you will be credited with full marks.

**(c) Describe, and use your biological knowledge to explain, the shape of the curve between the following concentrations of hydrogen peroxide:**
**(i)  5% and 15%**                                                               (2 marks)
**(ii) 15% and 20%**                                                              (2 marks)

e Notice that you have to do two things for each part of the question — you must *describe* the curve and *explain* it. Between 5% and 15%, there is a linear (regular) increase in the rate as more and more active sites become occupied at any one time. Between 15% and 20%, there is very little increase because all the active sites are occupied for most of the time.

**(d) Conclusions drawn from this graph may not be very reliable.**
   **Suggest and explain one reason why.** (2 marks)
   **Section A total: 17 marks**

ⓔ Once you see a question about reliability, you should be thinking about lack of repeats or inappropriate values for the IV. There is nothing that specifically indicates a lack of repeats in this investigation and since the y-axis is labelled 'mean volume of oxygen produced', some repeats were carried out. However, there are only four quite widely spaced values of the IV and there are no data for 0% (or for any value less than 5%) so what happens here is a complete guess.

# Section B

In Section B of the written test, you will be given resource materials related to the investigation you have carried out. These are often of an applied nature — that is, the concepts are in a real-life situation. For example, you could be given resource material about the activity of catalase in liver cells from humans.

## Resource sheet

### Resource A

Biologists investigated the relative catalase content of three cheeses:
- unpasteurised Cheddar cheese
- pasteurised Cheddar cheese
- Swiss Emmental cheese

The scientists cut a sample of cheese from the interior of a large block of unpasteurised Cheddar cheese.

They used a pestle and mortar to grind 5 grams of this sample of cheese with 25 grams of sand.

They placed this ground material in a large test tube.

They added $25\,cm^3$ of 1% hydrogen peroxide buffered to pH7 to the contents of the test tube.

They then placed the test tube in a water bath at 20°C.

They used a water-filled burette to collect the oxygen released from the test tube and recorded the volume released after 30 minutes.

They repeated this method several times with each type of cheese.

Their results are shown in the table.

| Sample number | Volume of oxygen released in 30 minutes/cm³ | | |
| --- | --- | --- | --- |
| | Unpasteurised Cheddar cheese | Pasteurised Cheddar cheese | Swiss Emmental cheese |
| 1 | 5.0 | 0.5 | 10.5 |
| 2 | 6.5 | 0.5 | 37.5 |
| 3 | 7.5 | 1.5 | 12.5 |
| 4 | 5.0 | 0.5 | 17.0 |
| 5 | 8.5 | 0.5 | 11.0 |
| 6 | 4.0 | 0.6 | 30.5 |
| 7 | 3.5 | 0.8 | 5.0 |
| 8 | 2.0 | 0.5 | 21.0 |
| 9 | 5.0 | | 24.0 |
| 10 | 8.0 | | 17.5 |
| 11 | 3.0 | | 19.0 |
| 12 | 6.0 | | 18.0 |
| 13 | 4.5 | | 28.5 |
| 14 | 6.0 | | 8.0 |
| Mean | | 0.675 | 18.6 |

## Resource B

Pasteurisation is a process that involves heat treatment and kills many harmful bacteria. Milk used in the production of cheese is often pasteurised. In the production of Swiss Emmental cheese, the milk is treated with hydrogen peroxide instead of by pasteurisation. Hydrogen peroxide is toxic to cells.

Residues of hydrogen peroxide in the milk would inhibit the bacterial cultures that are required for the production of Swiss Emmental cheese. These residues are removed by adding catalase enzyme to the milk. This enzyme converts the hydrogen peroxide to water and oxygen, which are harmless. The catalase was obtained traditionally from cattle livers.

A group of biologists investigated whether different bacteria could be used to make Swiss Emmental cheese. To measure catalase production, they incubated a sample of each type of bacterium in milk and recorded the volume of oxygen released from the milk in 30 minutes. Their results are shown in the table.

| Type of bacterium | Volume of oxygen produced in 30 minutes/cm³ |
| --- | --- |
| Type 1 | 0.0 |
| Type 2 | 0.0 |
| Type 3 | 0.0 |
| Type 4 | 0.0 |
| Type 5 | 48.7 |
| Type 6 | 0.0 |
| Type 7 | 0.0 |

Use the information in the **Resource sheet** to answer the questions.

Answer *all* questions in the space provided.

Use **Resource A** to answer questions 6 to 9.

**6   Calculate the mean volume of oxygen produced by unpasteurised Cheddar cheese.**                    (1 mark)

ⓔ A simple starter — just add up the volumes and divide by 14.

**7   List four variables that were controlled in the investigation.**                    (2 marks)

ⓔ You might think that this is 1 mark for two variables, but it is more likely to be marked
as follows: four correct = 2 marks, two or three correct = 1 mark, none or one correct = 0
marks. There are a number of controlled variables you could choose:
• mass of cheese
• mass of sand
• volume of hydrogen peroxide
• pH
• temperature
• time
• source of cheese (from the centre)

This should be an easy 2 marks.

**8   Compare the reliability of the data for Swiss Emmental cheese and
     unpasteurised Cheddar cheese.**                    (3 marks)

ⓔ The obvious points to make here are that the data for the Emmental cheese show a lot of
variation. There is a considerable range between highest and lowest, whereas results for the
unpasteurised Cheddar are closer together. However, you should consider not just the actual
differences — bigger numbers are likely to have bigger differences — but also the proportions
of one to the other. For example, the ratio of highest value to lowest value in the Cheddar
cheese data is 8.5:2.0 = 4.25. That's quite a high ratio. However, the ratio for the Emmental is
even higher at 7.5 (37.5:5.0). In this case, looking at these ratios supports what we found with
the raw data. In other cases it might not and you should point that out.

**9   The mean values for the three cheeses look very different.**
     **(a)  What other information would you require to be sure that there is a
          real difference between these means?**                    (1 mark)

ⓔ You would also need to know the standard deviations.

     **(b)  How would you use this information to decide whether or not the
          difference between the means was real?**                    (2 marks)

ⓔ You would need to know whether or not the standard deviations overlap. If they do, then
the differences are unlikely to be real. If they do not overlap, the differences are likely to be real.

Use **Resource B** to answer questions 10 to 13.

**10 Suggest why hydrogen peroxide can be used instead of pasteurisation in the production of cheese.** (2 marks)

> ⓔ You are told that hydrogen peroxide is toxic to cells. Presumably this means all cells, including those of any harmful bacteria in the milk. The hydrogen peroxide will kill these bacteria and sterilise the milk.

**11 Some of the flavour of Emmental cheese comes from the proteins in the milk used. Suggest why producers of Emmental prefer to use hydrogen peroxide rather than pasteurisation in the production of their cheese.** (3 marks)

> ⓔ Pasteurisation involves heating the milk. Heat denatures proteins and so pasteurisation could affect the flavour of the cheese. Using hydrogen peroxide will not affect the proteins and so will not affect the flavour.

**12 Explain why catalase is added to Emmental cheese.** (3 marks)

> ⓔ Catalase breaks down hydrogen peroxide into water and oxygen. If it were not added, the hydrogen peroxide would kill the bacteria that are added to the milk in the production of the cheese.

**13 Identify which type of bacterium would be suitable in the production of Swiss Emmental cheese and explain *one* advantage of using a bacterium in this process.** (2 marks)
**Section B total: 19 marks**

> ⓔ Type 5 would be suitable; it must produce a catalase since the hydrogen peroxide released oxygen. The use of bacteria would enable vegetarians, who would object to the use of catalase from the livers of cattle, to eat the cheese.

# The Unit 6 assessment
## What you must be able to do

This unit addresses the following aspects of the A2 subject criteria. The ability to:
- demonstrate and describe ethical, safe and skilful practical techniques, selecting appropriate qualitative and quantitative methods
- make, record and communicate reliable and valid observations and measurements with appropriate precision and accuracy
- analyse, interpret, explain and evaluate the methodology, results and impact of your own and others' experimental and investigative activities in a variety of ways

Candidates will be assessed on their understanding of investigative and practical skills in this unit and in Units 4 and 5. Opportunities to carry out practical work are provided in the context of material contained in Units 4 and 5.

**3.6.1 Investigating biological problems involves changing a specific factor, the independent variable, and measuring the changes in the dependent variable that result.**

The requirements here are identical to those for the Unit 3 assessment except for the following additional skill:
- Describe how you would collect a full range of useful quantitative data that could be analysed statistically.

**3.6.2 Implementing involves the ability to work methodically and safely, demonstrating competence in the required manipulative skills and efficiency in managing time. Raw data should be collected methodically and recorded during the course of the investigation.**

The requirements here are identical to those for the Unit 3 assessment.

**3.6.3 Data should be analysed by means of an appropriate statistical test. This allows calculation of the probability of an event being due to chance. Appropriate conclusions should be drawn and scientific knowledge from the A-level specification should be used to explain these conclusions.**

This means that you should be able to use your knowledge and understanding of the A2 specification in order to:
- select an appropriate statistical test from the following:
  - standard error and 95% confidence limits
  - Spearman rank correlation
  - $\chi^2$ test
- justify your choice of the statistical test
- construct an appropriate null hypothesis
- calculate the test statistic given a standard scientific calculator
- interpret the calculated test statistic in terms of:
  - the critical value at the 5% significance level ($p = 0.05$)
  - the probability of a result occurring by chance
  - acceptance or rejection of your null hypothesis
- draw valid conclusions, and use your biological knowledge and understanding of the A-level specification to explain and justify these conclusions

**3.6.4 Limitations are inherent in the material and apparatus used and procedures adopted. These limitations should be identified, evaluated and methods of overcoming them suggested.**

This means you should be able to:
- identify the limitations inherent in the apparatus and techniques used
- discuss and assess the relative effects of these limitations on the reliability and precision of the data and on the conclusions that may be drawn, resolving conflicting evidence
- suggest realistic ways in which the effect of these limitations may be reduced
- suggest further investigations that would provide additional evidence for the conclusions drawn

> **Examiner tip**
> Although there are many more statistical tests, these three are the only ones you are expected to be able to use in your A2 ISA or EMPA.

> **Examiner tip**
> Notice that the last statement refers to the A-level specification. This means that you could be asked to include your understanding of material from the AS units as well as from the A2 units.

# Unit 6 assessment: ISAs and EMPAs

There are two routes through which Unit 6 assessment can be delivered. They are:
- **ISA (Investigative Skills Assessment)** Your teachers mark your practical assessments and submit the marks, and a selection of work as examples, to a moderator who checks the marking.
- **EMPA (Externally Marked Practical Assignment)** All the practical work you complete is marked by examiners; none of it is marked by your teachers.

The components of the two assessments and their approximate mark allocations are shown in Table 24.

**Table 24**

| Assessment route | | | | |
|---|---|---|---|---|
| **ISA** | | **EMPA** | | |
| **Component** | **Marks** | **Component** | **Marks** | |
| Practical skills assessment: your teacher submits an assessment based on your practical skills throughout the course. | 6 | Practical skills verification: your teacher submits a verification of your practical skills, based on your work throughout the course. | 0 | |
| Task Stage 1: you carry out a task specified by AQA and record your results in a table. You have to decide on some aspects of the task yourself (e.g. controls, volumes, number of repeats). There are no marks for this part of the assessment at A2. | 0 | Task 1: you carry out a task specified by AQA. You have to decide on some aspects of the task yourself (e.g. controls, volumes, number of repeats). You answer questions about some aspects of the task. | 10 | |
| Task Stage 2: you begin an analysis of your data and carry out an appropriate statistical test. AQA supply guidance to help you: <br> • choose the test <br> • carry out the calculation | 6 | Task 2: you carry out a second, related task specified by AQA and record the results in a table that you construct. (0 marks) You begin an analysis of your data and carry out an appropriate statistical test. AQA supply guidance to help you: <br> • choose the test <br> • carry out the calculation (6 marks) | 6 | |
| Section A of written test: you answer questions based on the results from your own investigation. | 18 | Section A of written test: you answer questions based on the results from your own investigation. | 12 | |
| Section B of written test: you answer questions based on related material supplied by AQA. | 20 | Section B of written test: you answer questions based on related material supplied by AQA. | 22 | |
| Total for ISA | 50 | Total for EMPA | 50 | |

**Examiner tip**
During Task 2, your teacher will be provide you with a copy of the AQA *Students' Statistics Sheet*, which contains all the information you need to choose, calculate and evaluate your test statistic.

# The practical skills you will need

AQA assumes that you are familiar with the use of basic equipment, such as measuring cylinders, Bunsen burners, thermometers etc. as well as the skills developed in the AS course. But you must be able to show the following skills also.

## The use of a three-way tap in collecting gas samples

The apparatus shown in Figure 26 is a respirometer. It is used for measuring the rate of oxygen uptake by small, respiring organisms. One of the tubes contains the respiring organisms; the other acts as a 'thermobarometer'. Any changes in pressure and temperature that take place in the experimental tube (which would affect measurements of volumes), also take place in the thermobarometer tube and so are effectively cancelled out. The bung of each boiling tube is fitted with a three-way tap. This makes it possible to take repeat readings without having to reassemble the apparatus, and it also eliminates many of the leaks that could otherwise occur.

**Knowledge check 30**

Suggest why potassium hydroxide solution is present in both tubes in Figure 26.

Three-way tap

A

Plastic or metal cage containing glass beads

Potassium hydroxide solution

1 cm³ syringe

B

Plastic or metal cage containing seeds

Filter paper rolled to form a wick

Potassium hydroxide solution

Capillary U-tube containing coloured oil

**Figure 26** A simple respirometer

**Figure 27** How a three-way tap works

When the tap is in the position shown in Figure 27, the atmosphere and the boiling tube are connected. The position of the tap can be altered so that any two components are connected. By opening the three-way tap on tube A to the atmosphere and that on tube B to the syringe, and moving the barrel of the syringe, the pressure in the two tubes can be equalised.

# Establishing anaerobic conditions

**Knowledge check 31**

Which part, or parts, of cell respiration occur during anaerobic respiration?

In experiments involving fermentation (usually by yeast), it is important that anaerobic conditions are maintained throughout the investigation. The reason for this is that the rate of fermentation is usually measured by recording the rate of carbon dioxide production under different conditions. This is valid only if fermentation is the sole method of production of carbon dioxide.

The summary equation for fermentation in yeast is:

$$C_6H_{12}O_6 \rightarrow 2C_2H_5OH + 2CO_2$$

However, the summary equation for aerobic respiration in yeast is:

$$C_6H_{12}O_6 + 6O_2 \rightarrow 6H_2O + 6CO_2$$

Allowing aerobic respiration to occur introduces several potential errors. For example:
- Aerobic respiration gives three times as much carbon dioxide per molecule of glucose; so, if different amounts of aerobic respiration took place in different trials, the results would not be valid.
- Collecting the carbon dioxide produced often depends on the pressure of the carbon dioxide being able to force the gas through a delivery tube; with aerobic respiration, an equal volume of oxygen is absorbed by the yeast, so there is no overall change in pressure.

**Figure 28** Investigating anaerobic respiration in yeast

Figure 28 shows a simple way to investigate the rate of anaerobic respiration in yeast. To maintain anaerobic conditions, you must take two main precautions:

- Make up the glucose solution in boiled, cooled, distilled water.
- Once in the reaction vessel, with the yeast added, cover the surface of the liquid with a thin layer of oil or liquid paraffin (this prevents oxygen in the atmosphere entering the liquid).

# Random sampling

## Sampling populations

Investigating all the members of a population is only rarely possible. So to form a picture of what that population is like, we need a **representative** sample — a sample that is typical of the whole population.

How do we take a representative sample? This involves a circuitous argument because to take a truly representative sample we would have to know already what the population was like — for example, what percentage of the main types of individuals there were in the population — in order to include the same percentages in the sample. Since we do not know that, we must settle for an approximation. The best we can do is to take a random sample. In a **random sample** every individual has an equal chance of being included in the sample, so there is no bias.

You must appreciate, however, that a random sample does not *guarantee* a representative sample. Every individual has an equal probability of being included in the sample, so the sample *could* be made up of all the tallest plants, or all the heaviest mice. It is unlikely, but it could happen. In any case, it's our best shot at a representative sample.

Suppose you want to find the average height (or mass, or IQ, or handspan) of 400 17-year-olds. To create a random sample, you could:

- give each 17-year-old a number
- use a random number generator on a calculator or computer to generate a sample of (say) 50 numbers between 1 and 400
- measure each individual whose number was generated and work out the mean

The same principle could apply to any population.

To improve reliability, you could:

- take three random samples, make measurements of the desired feature, calculate the mean in each sample and calculate the mean of the means
- take one larger sample

## Sampling areas

To estimate the abundance of each species in an area, you would:

- estimate the abundance in several sample areas
- calculate the mean abundance
- multiply this by the ratio of the whole area to that of the sample area

**Knowledge check 32**

Making up a glucose solution with boiled, cooled distilled water maintains anaerobic conditions. Explain why.

**Examiner tip**

Carbon dioxide can still escape through the oil/liquid paraffin because it is at higher pressure than the atmosphere.

A **sample** is a subset of a population.

**Bias** occurs when a biologist selects where to take samples because 'they look typical'. The biologist's perception of what is typical might be misinformed and so the sample might not be a representative sample — it might not be typical of the whole population.

**Examiner tip**

Rather than use a random number generator, you could pull numbers out of a hat.

A **quadrat frame** is the equipment you use to mark out the area to be sampled. A **quadrat** is the area within the quadrat frame.

The abundance of organisms in an area is usually estimated by using **quadrat frames**. The **quadrat** forms the sample area. Quadrat frames come in different styles and sizes. The simplest is a square metal frame, which you place on the ground and estimate the abundance of the organisms inside the quadrat frame. Figure 29 shows how to place quadrat frames at random.

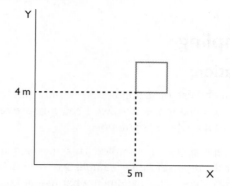

**Figure 29** Placing a quadrat frame at random

A single number is not enough to define the position of the quadrat frame — we need two. What we must do is:

- divide the area into a grid and number the coordinates on each side of the grid
- use the random number generator on a calculator to produce a pair of coordinates, for example X5, Y4 (this pair would define the bottom left-hand corner of the square on the diagram)
- place a quadrat frame with its bottom left-hand corner on the intersection of the coordinates
- estimate the abundance of the different organisms inside the quadrat
- repeat several times and calculate the mean

## Collecting reliable ecological data

Ecological investigations are usually aimed at finding out something along the following lines:

- What types of organisms are found here?
- How abundant are they?
- Where are they most abundant within the area?
- What abiotic factors might be responsible for the distribution?

To find the answers to these questions, some or all of the following must be measured or estimated:

- size of populations
- distribution of organisms
- values for the abiotic factors

**Knowledge check 33**

What type of factors are abiotic factors?

### Estimating population density (the size of a population)

*Estimating the number of plants and small non-mobile animals*

- Place quadrat frames randomly as described above.
- Count the number of organisms of the species you are investigating in each sample quadrat.

- Find the mean number per quadrat.
- Estimate the population size using the formula:

$$\frac{\text{mean number of organisms per quadrat} \times \text{area of field}}{\text{area per quadrat}}$$

It is important that you use the same units for the area of the field and the area of the quadrat (e.g. both in $cm^2$ or both in $m^2$).

## Estimating the percentage cover of plants and small, non-mobile animals

Sometimes, it is extremely difficult to count the number of organisms, even in the small area of a quadrat. How many blades of grass belong to each plant, for example?

**Figure 30** A quadrat frame subdivided into 25 squares

To get around this, biologists sometimes estimate the **percentage cover** of a species. For example, if the organism takes up half of the quadrat, then the percentage cover is 50%. A better way of estimating percentage cover is to use a quadrat frame that is subdivided into smaller squares.

The quadrat frame shown in Figure 30 has 25 smaller squares; each square is 4% of the total area.

If the species covers 7 squares, the percentage cover is 7 × 4% = 28%.

## Estimating the frequency of plants and small, non-mobile animals

Another method of estimating abundance is to measure the **frequency** of the species. This is the proportion of quadrats in which a species is found, expressed as a percentage. The advantages of using frequency as a measure are that it is easy and fast, and does not involve subjective judgments, which percentage cover can (since you must judge how much of the quadrat, or square within a quadrat, is covered).

One major disadvantage of using frequency is that results are not only affected by abundance of the species, but also by how it is distributed. For example, two species that are equally abundant will have different frequencies if one species is clumped and the other species is evenly distributed in the community. Figure 31 shows how this can occur.

Species A and species B have an identical population density of seven plants in the $36\,m^2$ area investigated. However, their frequencies are different.

**Examiner tip**
If a species only covers parts of squares in a quadrat frame like the one in Figure 30, you can roughly add them up. For example if a species covers 8 squares and 2 part-squares, then a total of 9 squares is a reasonable estimate. This would give 9 × 4 = 36% cover.

**Figure 31** Distribution of a species affects the frequency

Species A occurs in four of the 36 squares within the quadrat:

$$\text{frequency of species A} = \frac{4}{36} \times 100 = 11\%$$

Species B occurs in seven of the 36 squares within the quadrat:

$$\text{frequency of species B} = \frac{7}{36} \times 100 = 19\%$$

Another problem with using frequency to estimate abundance of a species is that the size of the quadrat used affects the results.

**Figure 32** The size of quadrat influences the estimate of frequency

Figure 32 is similar to Figure 31, except that the quadrats are larger.

Species A occurs in three of the nine squares within the quadrat:

$$\text{frequency of species A} = \frac{3}{9} \times 100 = 33\%$$

Species B occurs in five of the nine squares within the quadrat:

$$\text{frequency of species B} = \frac{5}{9} \times 100 = 56\%$$

These are very different results from those determined previously, and all that has changed is the size of the squares within the quadrat.

## Estimating the number of small, mobile animals

To estimate the size of a population of animals that move about, biologists use the **mark–release–recapture** technique. It is carried out in the following way.

- Collect a sample of the animals from the area and count them ($N_1$).
- Put a small mark, using a harmless substance in an unobtrusive place, on each animal. This is to ensure that the animal is not harmed by the process itself and that the marking does not affect its survival chances by making it more noticeable to predators.
- Release the marked animals and allow time for them to disperse among the population.
- Collect a second sample and note both the total size of the sample ($N_2$) and the number that are marked ($n$).

The assumption made now is that the proportion of the population collected in the first sample is the same as the proportion of marked individuals in the second sample. We can write this mathematically, as:

$$\frac{N_1}{X} = \frac{n}{N_2}$$

Rearranging the formula allows calculation of the population size:

$$X = \frac{(N_1 \times N_2)}{n}$$

### Assumptions in the mark–release–recapture technique

The following assumptions are made when using the mark–release–recapture technique. They are unlikely to be met fully.

- There are no migrations.
- There are no births.
- There are no deaths.
- Marking does not affect behaviour.
- On release, there is random mixing of the marked and unmarked individuals.
- The second sample is representative of the population as a whole.

Despite not being able to meet these assumptions, the technique gives a reasonable estimate of population size.

The reliability of the technique is affected by several factors. We can increase reliability by:

- using larger samples at both stages of the investigation
- allowing sufficient time for the released animals to mix (but not too long as they may then be more likely to migrate or die)
- repeating the investigation several times to obtain a mean

# Using a line transect to investigate the distribution of organisms in an area

- Lay a tape measure across the sample area.
- At regular intervals (every 4 m in the diagram) lay five quadrat frames to one side (always the same side) of the tape (Figure 33).

**Examiner tip**

Use a line transect if there is a clear change across the area you intend to investigate. The transition from a field to a wood, or from the low-tide region to the high-tide region of a rocky shore, are good examples of when you would use a line transect.

**Figure 33** Line transect

- Estimate the abundance of the different organisms at each sampling point along the transect by either:
  - recording presence or absence in each of the five quadrats and converting the number of occurrences to a **percentage frequency** (e.g. a species that occurs in four of the five quadrats has a frequency of 80%)
  - estimating the percentage of each quadrat covered by the species and taking the mean for the five quadrats to give the average **percentage cover**
  - counting the numbers of each organism in each quadrat to obtain a **mean number** for each sampling point

At each sample point, you should monitor the environmental factors that might influence the distribution of the organisms. These might include:

- light intensity
- soil pH
- soil water content
- nutrient availability in the soil

It might be possible to find a correlation between the abundance of an organism and one or more of the abiotic factors and analyse it using the Spearman rank correlation (see pages 75–77).

The distance between sampling points along the transect is important. If they are too far apart, species will be missed; if they are too close, it will be very time consuming and might yield too many data to be able to see patterns of zonation easily. Table 25 illustrates this point. It shows the number of species recorded for three different sampling intervals along two 20-metre transects at right angles to each other.

**Table 25**

| Sampling along transect | Number of species recorded | |
|---|---|---|
| | Line transect 1 N/S | Line transect 2 E/W |
| Continuous | 31 | 34 |
| Every metre | 15 | 17 |
| Every other metre | 9 | 12 |

**Knowledge check 36**

What effect has increasing the distance between sampling points in Table 25 had on estimating the distribution of species?

## Measuring abiotic factors

There are always reasons why a particular plant or animal is abundant (or not) in a certain area. These reasons are often linked to abiotic (environmental) factors. For example, some plants are extremely intolerant of an alkaline soil and will not grow well where the underlying rock is limestone (which gives rise to an alkaline soil). Water availability is another key factor for many plants; how many rose bushes grow in the Sahara desert?

There are some ground rules about taking readings of abiotic factors. You should bear in mind that a particular abiotic factor might change over the course of the investigation. Because of the rotation of the Earth, different parts of the area you are investigating could be in shade or in sunlight at different times of the day. Cloud cover might also change. Both these factors could influence light intensity. You need to be alert to this and take all readings in full sunlight (or all in shade, but the former is better). If you take readings of some parts of the area in full sunlight and others in shade (or when there is cloud cover) this particular variable will not have been controlled and your conclusions will not be valid.

If you see a dark cloud on the horizon, you might assume that it will rain before you can complete your investigation. You should collect any soil samples before it rains. Collecting the samples after the shower could have a major effect on your results and make your conclusions invalid.

# Specific investigations you need to know about

Besides the practical skills described, there are certain investigations you need to know about. It is unlikely that you will be asked to carry out the particular version of these investigations that you have carried out in your school or college. However, you might be asked to carry out, and comment on, an investigation testing the same relationship in a different context.

Table 26 lists those practicals that are identified in the specification.

**Table 26**

| Practical | Independent variable | Dependent variable | Controlled variables |
|---|---|---|---|
| Effect of light intensity on the rate of photosynthesis | Light intensity | Rate of photosynthesis | Carbon dioxide concentration, temperature |
| Effect of carbon dioxide concentration on the rate of photosynthesis | Carbon dioxide concentration | Rate of photosynthesis | Temperature, light intensity |
| Effect of temperature on the rate of photosynthesis | Temperature | Rate of photosynthesis | Carbon dioxide concentration, light intensity |
| *The above investigations are examples of the specification requirement that 'candidates should carry out investigations into the effect of a specific limiting factor on the rate of photosynthesis'.* | | | |
| Effect of temperature on the respiration of yeast | Temperature | Rate of respiration | Nature of substrate, substrate concentration, volume of substrate, mass of yeast, aerobic/anaerobic conditions |
| Effect of nature of substrate on the respiration of yeast | Substrate, e.g. type of carbohydrate | Rate of respiration | Temperature, substrate concentration, volume of substrate, mass of yeast, aerobic/ anaerobic conditions |
| Effect of temperature on the respiration of a larger organism (e.g. an insect) | Temperature | Rate of respiration | Mass of organisms, volume of air in respirometer |
| *The above investigations are examples of the requirement that 'candidates should carry out investigations into the effect of a specific variable on the respiration of a suitable organism'.* | | | |
| Ecological investigation into the effect of an abiotic factor on the numbers of organisms in different areas | Abiotic factor, e.g. soil pH, soil water content, light intensity | Frequency or % cover of the organism in the two areas | Other abiotic factors should be monitored |
| Ecological investigation into the effect of an abiotic factor on the distribution of organisms along a transect | Abiotic factor, e.g. soil pH, soil water content, light intensity | Frequency or % cover of the organism at points along the transect | Other abiotic factors should be monitored |

# Other skills you will need

You will need all the 'other skills' described for the Unit 3 assessment. You will also have to be able to select an appropriate statistical test, calculate the test value from your data and interpret your calculated values in terms of probability and chance.

## Selecting and using an appropriate statistical test

The statistical test is a means of assessing the probability of patterns in results having a biological cause or just being due to chance events. You will have to:

- choose a statistical test appropriate to the investigation
- calculate the test statistic
- interpret your calculated value in terms of probability and chance

This might sound daunting but, in the ISA (or EMPA), you will be given guidance on:

- which test to use
- how to calculate the test statistic

To help you choose an appropriate statistical test, AQA provides a *Students' Statistics Sheet*. It includes the decision tree shown in Figure 34.

**Figure 34** The *Students' Statistics Sheet* decision tree

You need to appreciate:

- the need for a statistical analysis of results
- how to interpret the value of the test statistic once you have calculated it
- that **probability** is a mathematical term which expresses the likelihood of an event occurring

The process of statistical analysis was started in Unit 3 where standard deviations about the mean were used to give an idea of the variability of data. It was noted that if the standard deviations of two mean values of the DV (for different values of the IV) overlap, then we cannot be certain that there is a real difference between those two means.

**Examiner tip**
You must express a probability as a decimal fraction of one. For example, an event that is likely to occur 5 times in every 100 trials has a probability of 0.05.

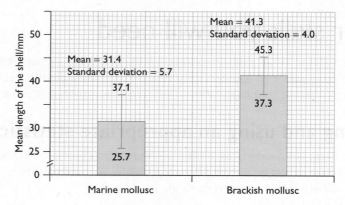

**Figure 35** Shell length in molluscs

Figure 35 summarises measurements made on the shell length of two species of snail. For each species, the bar chart shows:

- the mean length of the shell
- the standard deviation (shown as bars above and below the mean)

If you look carefully, you will see that the standard deviations do not overlap — it's a close call, but they don't. Therefore, we can be reasonably confident that there is a statistically significant difference between the two mean values. Now look at Figure 36. This bar chart shows the numbers of invertebrates per $dm^3$ found at three sites in an English lake.

**Figure 36**

The standard deviations for all three sites overlap, so we cannot be confident that there is a statistically significant difference between the numbers.

What is meant by confident in this context? It is not sufficient to look at the means and say 'I'm pretty confident they are different!' We are talking about statistical confidence; personal opinion is irrelevant.

All statistical tests are designed to test whether or not there is either an association or a statistical difference between two (or more) conditions. We begin from the point that there is *no* statistical difference between the conditions. This is called a **null hypothesis**. The null hypothesis is the opposite of what you would expect to happen. An **alternate hypothesis** for what you expect to happen can be stated in one of two ways:

A **null hypothesis** states that there will be *no* difference between two samples or between the values of the dependent variable measured at two different values of the independent variable. In experiments, we seek to disprove a null hypothesis.

- **non-directional** — a change in factor A brings about a change in factor B
- **directional** — an increase in factor A brings about an increase in factor B; an increase in factor A brings about a decrease in factor B

Table 27 contains some examples of null hypotheses, together with the corresponding alternative hypotheses.

**Table 27**

| Null hypothesis | Alternative hypothesis | |
| | Non-directional | Directional |
| --- | --- | --- |
| There will be no difference in abundance of buttercups growing in an acid soil and in an alkaline soil. | There will be a difference in abundance between buttercups growing in an acid soil and in an alkaline soil. | There will be more buttercups growing in an acid soil than in an alkaline soil. |
| A change in temperature will have no effect on the activity of catalase. | A change in temperature will affect the activity of catalase. | An increase in temperature will increase the activity of catalase (up to an optimum temperature). |
| There will be no difference in size of leaves of nettle plants growing in full sunlight and those growing in shade. | The leaves of nettle plants growing in full sunlight will differ in size from those growing in shade. | The leaves of nettle plants growing in full sunlight will be smaller than those growing in shade. |
| The type of sugar used will have no effect on the rate of anaerobic respiration in yeast. | Different sugars will be fermented at different rates by yeast. | Glucose will be fermented faster than sucrose by yeast. |

Statistics do not deal in certainties, only in probabilities. We can never be certain that a particular null hypothesis should be accepted or rejected. Statistical tests enable us to say, with a certain level of probability, that 'either there are, or there are not'. The level of probability that is commonly used in biology is the 5% probability level, often written as $p = 0.05$. When you calculate a particular test statistic (whatever it may be), there is a certain value of that statistic that corresponds to $p = 0.05$. This is called the **critical value** and can be found from probability tables. Your calculated value may be greater than, equal to or less than the critical value. You should interpret these outcomes as described below.

- If the calculated value is equal to, or greater than, the critical value for $p = 0.05$, there is a less than 5% probability that these are just random variations; they are therefore likely to have a biological cause. You reject the null hypothesis.
- If the calculated value is less than the critical value for $p = 0.05$, there is a greater than 5% probability that the results represent random events. You cannot be confident of a biological cause for any differences; you must accept the null hypothesis.

This is summarised in Table 28.

**Table 28**

| Hypothesis | Test value equal to or greater than critical value | Test value less than critical value |
| --- | --- | --- |
| Null hypothesis | Reject | Accept |
| Alternative hypothesis | Accept | Reject |

**Examiner tip**

If your statistical test shows that the probability of the differences in your results occurring by chance is equal to, or less than, 0.05, you should reject your null hypothesis.

**Examiner tip**

For our purposes, the critical value is always the value for $p = 0.05$ (the 5% probability level).

**Examiner tip**
Use the standard error and 95% confidence limits to compare the means of two sets of data.

# Standard error and 95% confidence limits

Suppose you took a sample of the 17-year-olds in your school and found the mean height. Someone else takes another sample and also finds the mean height. Their sample will almost certainly be different from yours and their mean will be slightly different. So who is right? Well, both of you and neither of you! Without including everyone in the target population, we cannot be certain of the true mean. However, we can estimate the range of values within which the true mean lies. All we need is the mean (already calculated) and the standard deviation, which we can obtain by entering the data into a scientific calculator and pressing the SD button. Standard error is a measure of the variability, not of the raw data, but of the mean itself. It is calculated from the formula:

$$SE = \frac{s}{\sqrt{n}}$$

where

$SE$ = standard error

$s$ = standard deviation

$n$ = sample size/number of measurements

The standard error tells us that 68% of the time the mean will fall within the range corresponding to the calculated mean ± the standard error.

Consider an investigation into the reaction times of two groups of individuals. The null hypothesis is:

'There is no difference in reaction time between group 1 and group 2'.

Figure 37 shows the mean and standard error of reaction times in two groups.

**Figure 37** Reaction times in two groups of individuals with bars showing ± 1 standard error

**Examiner tip**
If you use the standard error and 95% confidence limits in your ISA or EMPA, simply multiply the standard error by 2.

Figure 37 tells us that 68% of the time, the mean reaction times of these two groups will fall within the range of values shown on the bar chart. However, our statistic does not mention 68% — it's all about 95% confidence limits. How do we get from 68% to 95%? Easy — we use a range of values equal to 1.96 times the standard error (twice is all right for your ISA or EMPA).

**Figure 38** The data from Figure 37 with bars showing ±2 standard errors

Figure 38 shows the same bar chart with the 95% intervals plotted. This time, the error bars represent the range of values within which the true mean will lie in 95% of cases. These are the 95% confidence limits.

The error bars in Figure 38 overlap, so we *cannot* be confident that the means are significantly different.

The way to report this is to say that the probability of the difference in the two means being due to chance is greater than 5% ($p > 0.05$). Consequently, we accept the null hypothesis (that there is no difference in the reaction times of the two groups).

## The chi-squared ($\chi^2$) test

This test is used to compare frequencies of organisms, to see whether or not the number of organisms in one category is significantly different from the number in another category. More specifically, $\chi^2$ tests whether or not the observed numbers differ from the numbers that would be expected if the organisms were distributed equally between two (or more) categories.

Suppose we want to know whether or not there are the same numbers of earthworms in two similar-sized fields. The null hypothesis would be:

'There is no difference in the number of worms in field A and field B.'

To test this, we would collect equal volumes of soil from several sites in each field and count the number of worms in each. Suppose the numbers were:

- Field A sample — 167 worms
- Field B sample — 198 worms

How many worms would there be in each field if the numbers found were distributed equally between the two fields?

$$\text{expected numbers} = \frac{(167 + 198)}{2} = 182.5$$

(You'll just have to live with the idea of half a worm!)

We now have all the information needed to calculate $\chi^2$:
- observed values ($O$, the number of worms counted)
- expected values ($E$, the number expected if the worms were distributed equally)

**Examiner tip**
Use the $\chi^2$ test when comparing the number of organisms in two or more categories. You can only use this test with raw data; you cannot use it with processed data, such as means or percentages.

To calculate $\chi^2$ we use the formula:

$$\chi^2 = \Sigma \frac{O - E^2}{E} \qquad (\Sigma \text{ means 'sum of'})$$

Table 29 shows a completed $\chi^2$ table for this investigation.

**Table 29**

| Number of worms | Observed (O) | Expected (E) | (O − E) | (O − E)² | $\frac{(O - E)^2}{E}$ |
|---|---|---|---|---|---|
| Field A | 167 | 182.5 | −15.5 | 240.25 | 1.32 |
| Field B | 198 | 182.5 | 15.5 | 240.25 | 1.32 |

The value of $\chi^2$ is given by adding together the two figures in the last column. Here:

$$\chi^2 = 1.32 + 1.32 = 2.64$$

**Examiner tip**

When using a table of $\chi^2$ values, the number of degrees of freedom is always 1 less than the number of categories being compared.

If the calculated value is equal to or greater than the critical value, the null hypothesis will be rejected and the conclusion will be that there is a genuine difference in the number of worms in the two fields. First, you need to know about the idea of **degrees of freedom**. This is linked to the number of categories compared in the $\chi^2$ calculation. The number of degrees of freedom is always one less than the number of categories. In this case, there are two categories (Field A and Field B) and so there is just one degree of freedom.

Look at Table 30. For this investigation, read across from 1 degree of freedom.

**Table 30**

| Degrees of freedom | Critical values at probability (p) = | | | | | | | | | |
|---|---|---|---|---|---|---|---|---|---|---|
| | 0.90 | 0.80 | 0.70 | 0.50 | 0.30 | 0.20 | 0.10 | 0.05 | 0.01 | 0.001 |
| 1 | 0.02 | 0.06 | 0.15 | 0.46 | 1.07 | 1.64 | 2.71 | 3.84 | 6.64 | 10.83 |
| 2 | 0.21 | 0.45 | 0.71 | 1.39 | 2.41 | 3.22 | 4.60 | 5.99 | 9.21 | 13.82 |
| 3 | 0.58 | 1.01 | 1.42 | 2.37 | 3.66 | 4.64 | 6.25 | 7.82 | 11.34 | 16.27 |
| 4 | 1.06 | 1.65 | 2.20 | 3.36 | 4.88 | 5.99 | 7.78 | 9.49 | 13.28 | 18.47 |
| 5 | 1.61 | 2.34 | 3.00 | 4.35 | 6.06 | 7.29 | 9.24 | 11.07 | 15.09 | 20.52 |
| 6 | 2.20 | 3.07 | 3.83 | 5.35 | 7.23 | 8.56 | 10.64 | 12.59 | 16.81 | 22.46 |
| 7 | 2.83 | 3.82 | 4.67 | 6.35 | 8.38 | 9.80 | 12.02 | 14.07 | 18.48 | 24.32 |
| 8 | 3.49 | 4.59 | 5.53 | 7.34 | 9.52 | 11.03 | 13.36 | 15.51 | 20.09 | 26.12 |
| 9 | 4.17 | 5.38 | 6.39 | 8.34 | 10.66 | 12.24 | 14.68 | 16.92 | 21.67 | 27.88 |
| 10 | 4.86 | 6.18 | 7.27 | 9.34 | 11.78 | 13.44 | 15.99 | 18.31 | 23.21 | 29.59 |
| | Not significant | | | | | | | Significant | | |

Our calculated value is 2.64. This falls between 1.64 (the value for $p = 0.20$) and 2.71 (the value for $p = 0.10$). As our value for $\chi^2$ is less than the value for $p = 0.05$, we must accept the null hypothesis. There is no significant difference in the numbers of earthworms in the two fields. The difference between the samples is due to chance.

$\chi^2$ does not limit you to comparing just two conditions. You could compare the numbers of worms in, say, seven fields equally well.

# The Spearman rank correlation

This test is used to test for associations between different measurements made from the same sample. For example, if we measure the height of several buttercup plants in the same field, and then find the pH of the soil the plants are growing in, we are using the same sample area to obtain two sets of different measurements.

**Examiner tip**
Use the Spearman rank correlation test when looking for an association between two different measurements made on the same sample.

The Spearman rank correlation is suitable for paired data that can be ranked from the highest value to the lowest value. We lay out the data in pairs and then:

- rank each set of data
- find the difference between the two ranks for each pair of values (it does not matter whether the difference is positive or negative)
- square the difference in ranks
- sum the squares of the differences

An example is given in Table 31.

**Table 31**

| Sample | Height of plant/cm | Rank 1 | pH of soil | Rank 2 | Rank difference (rank 2 − rank 1 = D) | Rank difference squared (D²) |
|--------|-------------------|--------|------------|--------|----------------------------------------|------------------------------|
| 1 | 27.5 | 2 | 6.3 | 9 | 7 | 49 |
| 2 | 18.0 | 7 | 7.2 | 3 | −4 | 16 |
| 3 | 11.0 | 10 | 7.6 | 1 | −9 | 81 |
| 4 | 22.5 | 3 | 6.4 | 8 | 5 | 25 |
| 5 | 29.5 | 1 | 6.8 | 6.5 | 5.5 | 30.25 |
| 6 | 16.5 | 8 | 7.0 | 5 | −3 | 9 |
| 7 | 19.0 | 5.5 | 6.0 | 10 | 4.5 | 20.25 |
| 8 | 13.5 | 9 | 6.8 | 6.5 | −2.5 | 6.25 |
| 9 | 21.0 | 4 | 7.4 | 2 | −2 | 4 |
| 10 | 19.0 | 5.5 | 7.1 | 4 | −1.5 | 2.25 |
| | | | | | | $\Sigma D^2 = 243$ |

**Examiner tip**
Note that the heights of the buttercup plants in Table 31 have been ranked from highest to lowest and then the pH values have been ranked from highest to lowest. The rank difference has been calculated between the pair of ranks across each row of the table.

We can now put this value into the formula for Spearman rank correlation, which is:

$$r_s = 1 - \frac{6 \times \Sigma(D)^2}{n^3 - n}$$

where

$r_s$ = Spearman rank correlation coefficient

$n$ = the number of pairs of items in the sample

$D$ = the difference between each pair of ranked measurements

Substituting into the formula gives:

$$r_s = 1 - \frac{6 \times 243}{10^3 - 10}$$

$$= 1 - \frac{1458}{990} = 1 - 1.47 = -0.47$$

Figure 39 should help to explain what a correlation of −0.47 means.

**Examiner tip**

If your calculated value for the Spearman rank correlation coefficient is greater than +1 or less than −1, you have made a mistake and should check your maths.

The value for the Spearman rank correlation coefficient always lies on this scale. The graphs in Figure 40 give an illustration of what is meant by perfect positive correlation, perfect negative correlation and no correlation.

**Figure 39**

**Figure 40**

However, the value of the coefficient does not tell us a lot. Our calculated value of −0.47 indicates a moderate negative correlation (i.e. buttercups grow taller when the pH is lower, but is the correlation significant? We need to check the result in probability tables (Table 32) for the appropriate number of degrees of freedom.

**Table 32**

| Number of pairs of measurements | Critical value for $p = 0.05$ |
|---|---|
| 5 | 1.00 |
| 6 | 0.89 |
| 7 | 0.79 |
| 8 | 0.74 |
| 9 | 0.68 |
| 10 | 0.65 |
| 12 | 0.59 |
| 14 | 0.54 |
| 16 | 0.51 |
| 18 | 0.48 |
| 20 | 0.46 |

**Examiner tip**

For the Spearman rank correlation, the number of degrees of freedom is two less than the number of pairs (because the data are in pairs).

In our example, there are ten pairs of measurements, so there are eight degrees of freedom. The critical value for $p = 0.05$ and eight degrees of freedom is 0.74 (the sign does not matter — it's just the size of the number).

The value −0.47 is less than the critical value, so the null hypothesis is accepted — at $p = 0.05$, there is no significant correlation between height of buttercups and soil pH.

Another way to check the significance of the Spearman rank correlation is to plot the value on a graph like that shown in Figure 41 and see if it falls above or below the appropriate critical value.

**Figure 41**

For a given number of degrees of freedom, any value that falls to the left of the curve (or underneath it, if you prefer) represents a non-significant correlation. If it falls on the curve or to the right of it (above it), there is a significant correlation at $p = 0.05$.

# What might a Unit 6 ISA (or EMPA) task look like?

## A2 Biology ISA (EMPA) Biol6 Task Sheet

*Factors affecting the growth of photosynthetic organisms*

### Introduction

You are required to investigate the abundance of one photosynthetic organism growing in two different conditions of light intensity. Your teacher will tell you which organism you will be investigating.

In the investigation you should collect reliable quantitative data measured to an appropriate level of accuracy.

You should decide what statistical test you intend to use.

You should then collect data that can be analysed statistically.

When collecting data you should decide for yourself:
- what measurements to make
- how to select your samples
- how many samples to take
- the relevant factors you will need to control or monitor

In the next stage you will analyse your results with a suitable statistical test.

You will then have to design an investigation.

Suppose you had been told to investigate the abundance of buttercups in two different areas of a field, one area in direct sunlight for most of the day and the other in shade for most of the day.

There are a number of steps to follow when designing such an investigation.

# Steps to follow

## Devise a method of random sampling of the two areas

The best method for this was discussed on p. 62. Lay two tape measures at right-angles to each other and use a random number generator to produce the coordinates for each quadrat.

## Decide how to measure abundance

Because buttercup plants are easily distinguished, there are three options. You could:
- count the number in each quadrat
- estimate the percentage cover in each quadrat
- calculate the frequency in each area

In this particular case, none of these would take long. It is probably best to go for the option that gives the most reliable information — counting the plants.

## Decide how many samples to take

This is best done by using the 'running mean' technique. As you carry out the investigation, you plot a graph of the mean abundance against the total number of samples taken. The x-axis is the number of samples (1, 2, 3 etc.) and the y-axis is the mean number of individuals per sample.

As the number of samples increases the running mean should begin to stabilise. Once this happens, you need only take a few more samples to be relatively confident of having a reasonably representative sample.

## Find the mean light intensity in the two areas

You need not necessarily take a light intensity reading at every sample point. However, as it is so quick to do, it is probably a good idea. On other occasions it may be more time-consuming and you would have to think of a reasonable compromise between reliability and practicality.

## Consider monitoring environmental factors such as soil pH and soil water content

In an ecological investigation, you cannot easily control variables that might influence the outcome. Therefore, you must monitor them. This is likely to form the basis of a question in Section A of the written test.

## Choose your statistical test at the outset

This is because it will influence the way in which you organise your data.

At the end of your investigation, you will have mean values for the abundance of buttercups in the two areas. Referring to the *Students' Statistics Sheet*, you should choose standard error and 95% confidence limits.

## After the investigation

- Carry out the statistical analysis of the results on your *Candidate Results Sheet* using the AQA *Students' Statistics Sheet*.

### Candidate Results Sheet: Stage 1

Record your data in a table in the space below.

Hand in this sheet at the end of each practical session.

There are no marks awarded for the table at A2.

*(Suppose you had the results shown in the table below.)*

| Quadrat number | Number of buttercups per quadrat | |
| --- | --- | --- |
| | Area in direct sunlight | Area in shade |
| 1 | 6 | 5 |
| 2 | 8 | 7 |
| 3 | 7 | 3 |
| 4 | 9 | 2 |
| 5 | 4 | 4 |
| 6 | 6 | 6 |
| 7 | 7 | 8 |
| 8 | 7 | 4 |
| 9 | 9 | 5 |
| 10 | 8 | 7 |
| 11 | 5 | 8 |
| 12 | 5 | 8 |
| 13 | 7 | 5 |
| 14 | 11 | 5 |
| 15 | 7 | 4 |
| 16 | 7 | 6 |
| 17 | 5 | 6 |

| 18 | 9 | 7 |
| 19 | 11 | 2 |
| 20 | 14 | 0 |

## Candidate Results Sheet: Stage 2

Analyse your data with a suitable statistical test. You may use a calculator and the AQA *Students' Statistics Sheet* that has been provided.

You are provided with a sheet of graph paper. You may use this if you wish.

Hand in this sheet at the end of the practical session.

**1  State your null hypothesis.** (1 mark)

ⓔ The null hypothesis is: 'there is no difference in the abundance of buttercups in the light and shaded areas of the field'.

**2  (a)  Give your choice of statistical test.** (1 mark)

ⓔ The test to use is standard error and 95% confidence limits.

**(b)  Give a reason for your choice of statistical test.** (1 mark)

ⓔ This test is chosen because two mean values are to be compared.

**3  Carry out the test and calculate the test statistic. Show your working.** (1 mark)

| Statistic | Number of buttercups per quadrat | |
| --- | --- | --- |
| | Area in direct sunlight | Area in shade |
| Mean | 7.60 | 5.10 |
| Standard deviation | 2.40 | 2.20 |

$$SE = \frac{s}{\sqrt{n}}$$

In both cases, $n = 20$, so $\sqrt{n} = 4.472$

| Statistic | Number of buttercups per quadrat | |
| --- | --- | --- |
| | Area in direct sunlight | Area in shade |
| Standard error | 0.54 | 0.49 |
| 2 × standard error | 1.08 | 0.98 |
| 95% confidence limits (mean ± 2 × standard error) | 6.52 – 8.68 | 4.12 – 6.08 |

**Examiner tip**
You would calculate the standard deviation by entering the data in your standard scientific calculator and pressing the SD button. There is no need to show any further working.

**Figure 42**

> 4 **Interpret the test statistic in relation to your null hypothesis. Use the words *probability* and *chance* in your answer.**
>
> (2 marks)

ⓔ From the table we can see that the 95% confidence limits do not overlap. Therefore, the probability of the difference between the two means being due to chance is less than 5% and we reject the null hypothesis.

# The written test

In Section A of the ISA (or EMPA) written test, you will have to answer questions about your investigation, or results based on a similar investigation.

## Section A

These questions are about your investigation into the effect of aspect on the abundance of an organism growing in two different light intensities. You should use the task sheet, your results and the statistical calculations you have carried out to answer the following questions.

Answer all questions in the space provided.

Name of the organism studied: buttercup

> I **Describe how you measured the abundance of the organism in each of the two conditions you studied.**
>
> (2 marks)

ⓔ An answer such as 'Quadrats were placed at random in the two areas using pairs of random coordinates generated by a scientific calculator' would make the point about randomness and also explain how this was achieved.

> 2 **How many samples did you take to estimate the abundance of the organism you studied? Explain why you took this number of samples.**
>
> (2 marks)

(e) This is a standard question. A suitable answer is: 20 samples were taken in each area — this is sufficient to allow a statistical analysis. You must explain that you have taken enough samples to allow statistical analysis.

**3** **Explain how you ensured that your samples were free from bias.** (1 mark)

(e) This touches on the same area again, but here you must stress that it is the random sampling that avoids bias.

**4** **Give two ways in which you ensured that the results from the two areas were comparable.** (2 marks)

(e) This is the 'fair test' idea. You need to be able to show that you have carried out the same procedure in both situations. So, you could quote, for example:
- same-sized quadrats
- same number of samples
- random samples

**5** **Describe how you monitored *two* environmental factors (other than light) during your investigation.** (2 marks)

(e) Here you have to describe how to monitor any two factors such as:
- soil pH
- soil moisture content

You should describe where you took the samples — that is to say from each quadrat or from other randomly selected sites in the areas — and how you would test for the environmental factor.

**6** **Other than light intensity, give *two* factors that could influence the growth of the organisms in the two conditions. Explain how each factor could influence growth.** (4 marks)

(e) You could use the factors you described in answer to question 5. However, although it is easy to test soil pH, it is less easy to explain the effect of soil pH. You could link water content to hydration of cells and temperature to any metabolic process, including photosynthesis.

**7** **The size of the quadrats you used could have influenced the reliability of your results. Describe *one* other way in which your procedure could have influenced the reliability of the results.** (2 marks)

**Section A total: 15 marks**

(e) There are several factors that could be mentioned here. Reliability is always influenced by the number of repeats — in this case, the number of samples. Human error could be a factor in deciding just what constitutes one buttercup plant, while the position of the quadrats, although random, may not be representative — they may have all been placed (because of the particular random coordinates) in an area that was particularly dense in buttercups.

# Section B

In Section B of the written test, you will be given several pieces of resource material that are related to the investigation you have carried out. These are often of an applied nature — that is, the concepts will be in a real-life situation.

## Resource sheet

### Resource A: Growing tomato plants (procedure)

Scientists divided 36 tomato plants into three groups of 12. They placed each of the groups on a separate bench in a greenhouse, where the individual plants were surrounded by moist sand (afterwards kept moistened), to a depth of 5 inches. They maintained a 14-hour day for all the plants, using a 1000 watt electric lamp. They illuminated each of the groups of plants with different light intensities using cheesecloth suspended 50 cm above the plants. The relative intensities they used were:

- 100% (no shade)
- 50.4% (one layer of cheesecloth)
- 22.3% (two layers of cheesecloth)

The scientists monitored humidity, air temperature, and soil temperature in each of the conditions. They allowed only five clusters of fruit to develop on each plant.

### Resource B: the effect of light intensity on leaf area of tomato plants

The scientists measured the leaf area of each tomato plant. The table summarises their data.

| Time/ days | Mean leaf area/cm$^2$ | | | Mean daily increase in leaf area since previous reading/cm$^2$ | | |
|---|---|---|---|---|---|---|
| | No shade | 1 layer of cheesecloth | 2 layers of cheesecloth | No shade | 1 layer of cheesecloth | 2 layers of cheesecloth |
| 0 | 1350 | 1503 | 1625 | – | – | – |
| 7 | 1649 | 2253 | 2473 | 42.7 | 107.1 | 121.1 |
| 11 | 1888 | 2684 | 3122 | 59.8 | 107.8 | 162.3 |
| 14 | 2088 | 2984 | 3594 | 66.7 | 100.0 | 157.3 |
| 18 | 2358 | 3408 | 4202 | 67.5 | 106.0 | 152.0 |
| 21 | 2668 | 3646 | 4694 | 102.8 | 79.3 | 164.0 |
| 25 | 3188 | 3901 | 5294 | 130.0 | 63.8 | 150.0 |
| 32 | 3754 | 4303 | 6259 | 80.9 | 57.4 | 137.9 |
| 39 | 4164 | 4680 | 6649 | 58.6 | 53.9 | 55.7 |
| 46 | 4325 | 5033 | 6764 | 23.0 | 50.4 | 16.4 |
| 53 | 4485 | 5433 | 6868 | 22.9 | 57.1 | 14.9 |
| 70 | 4563 | 5559 | 7072 | 4.6 | 7.4 | 12.0 |
| 100 | 4563 | 5559 | 7072 | 0.0 | 0.0 | 0.0 |

Resource C: the effect of light intensity on fruit production by tomato plants

The scientists also counted the number of fruits produced by the plants in each group and measured the mass of these fruits. The table summarises their data.

| Cluster of fruit | Total number of fruits from 12 plants | | | Mean mass of a single fruit/g | | |
| --- | --- | --- | --- | --- | --- | --- |
| | No shade | 1 layer of cheesecloth | 2 layers of cheesecloth | No shade | 1 layer of cheesecloth | 2 layers of cheesecloth |
| 1 | 57 | 29 | 0 | 58.5 | 54.2 | 0.0 |
| 2 | 75 | 54 | 20 | 78.2 | 67.2 | 77.7 |
| 3 | 58 | 57 | 39 | 90.9 | 71.2 | 70.9 |
| 4 | 61 | 47 | 56 | 95.0 | 82.9 | 82.0 |
| 5 | 20 | 18 | 27 | 87.9 | 80.4 | 70.8 |

Use the information in the **Resource sheet** to answer the questions.

Answer *all* questions in the space provided.

Use **Resource A** to answer questions 8 and 9.

**8** **Explain the advantage of using a 1000 watt electric light to illuminate the plants, rather than using natural daylight.**

(2 marks)

The 1000 watt electric light is controllable. The scientists can position it at a set distance from the plants to ensure equal lighting. It also gives a constant light intensity. It is switchable, so the scientists can control the light period. Each of these factors increases the reliability of the results, and will gain 1 mark.

**9** **Explain why the scientists used groups of 12 plants in the investigation.**

(2 marks)

**Examiner tip**
Remember the formula for calculating *any* percentage change is:

percentage change = change in value × 100/ original value

Be careful to get the emphasis correct here. It is important that the scientists used *groups*, rather than that the groups contained 12 plants. Groups allow us to calculate mean values (which are more representative) as well as to spot (and possibly exclude) any anomalous values, which increases reliability.

Use **Resource B** to answer questions 10 to 12.

**10** **Calculate the percentage increase in leaf area over the 100-day period for:**
**(a)  the plants with no shade**
**(b)  the plants shaded by two layers of cheesecloth**

(3 marks)

Two simple calculations are involved here:

change in value for plants with no shade = 4563 − 1350 = 3213 change in value for plants shaded by two layers of cheesecloth = 7072 − 1625 = 5447

% increase for the plants with no shade $= \dfrac{3213}{1350} \times 100 = 238.0$

% increase for the plants two layers of cheesecloth $= 5447 \times \dfrac{100}{1625} = 335.2$

**11 Describe the pattern of rate of growth of leaves for:**
   **(a) the plants with no shade**
   **(b) the plants shaded by two layers of cheesecloth** (4 marks)

To answer this question, you have to focus on the data concerning mean daily increase because this shows the rate of growth. The growth rate of the plants with no shade is initially low, rises to a maximum at day 25 and then decreases. The rate of growth of the plants shaded by two layers of cheesecloth is initially high and rises to a maximum by day 11. The high level of growth is sustained until day 32.

**12 The leaves of the plants shaded by layers of cheesecloth are bigger than those of plants with no shade.**
   **(a) Suggest *one* advantage to the shaded plants of this difference in leaf area.** (1 mark)

Bigger leaves have a larger surface area and so trap more light.

   **(b) A student concluded from these data that there was a significant difference in the mean area of leaves from plants shaded by two layers of cheesecloth and from those with no shade. Do you agree with his conclusion? Explain your answer.** (4 marks)

The student has judged that the differences are so large that they must be significant. However, he has not made reference to the time(s) at which he is making the comparison; he has not shown that he has carried out an appropriate statistical test; he has not provided an associated probability level to show that these differences are not due to chance.

   **(c) Is the difference in leaf area between the plants shaded by cheesecloth and the plants with no shade a measure of difference in their rates of growth? Explain your answer** (2 marks)

You need to think about this carefully. It is tempting to say that the plants with the bigger leaves must have grown both more and faster. However, the data are two-dimensional; they are concerned only with the area of the leaves — not the volume or mass. The leaves with the larger areas may well be thinner because there are fewer layers of cells. So there is not necessarily a correlation between leaf area and growth rate. (A moment's careful thought will tell you that this is unlikely; the plants with the smaller leaves are receiving less light than those with the larger leaves and so will photosynthesise less and grow less.)

Use **Resource C** to answer questions 13 to 15.

**13 Calculate the total number of fruits harvested from all 12 unshaded plants.** (1 mark)

ⓔ This could not be much simpler — just add them up! There are 271.

**14 Calculate the total mass of fruits harvested from the 12 unshaded plants.** (2 marks)

ⓔ This is another relatively simple calculation. For each group, the total mass equals:

number of fruits × mean fruit mass

Work this out for all five groups and add them together:

$(57 \times 58.5) + (75 \times 78.2) + (58 \times 90.9) + (61 \times 95.0) + (20 \times 87.9)$

= 22 024.7 g (Don't forget the units.)

**15 (a) Describe one piece of evidence which suggests that a higher light intensity results in a higher total mass of fruit.** (1 mark)

ⓔ In nearly all cases, both the number of fruit and the mean fruit mass are highest in the plants that have uncovered (unshaded) leaves. These receive the greatest light intensity.

**(b) Describe one piece of evidence that suggests that a higher light intensity does not result in a higher total mass of fruit.** (1 mark)

**Section B total: 23 marks**

ⓔ In group 5, the total mass of fruit is highest in the plants where the leaves were shaded by two layers of cheesecloth. You need to look carefully to find this information.

## Knowledge check answers

1 You could answer, 'I'm finding out whether temperature affects enzyme action', but that is not a prediction. 'Changing the temperature will affect the rate of the enzyme-controlled reaction' is a prediction. 'Changing the temperature will *not* affect the rate of enzyme-controlled reaction' is not only a prediction; it is a null hypothesis, which you can attempt to disprove by experimentation.

2 Any two from the following: temperature, air humidity, light intensity or length of time for which he exposed the jars.

3 He must have known that boiling kills microorganisms. In fact, he invented the process of pasteurisation, used to kill harmful microorganisms in, for example, milk.

4 However you worded your answer, you are likely to have described two principles. The use of mice might be valid because, like humans, they are mammals. The use of mice might not be valid because mice are rodents and humans are primates or because mice are genetically/physiologically different from humans.

5 These temperatures would be appropriate to find the range of temperatures in which the optimum temperature lies. You would need to repeat the experiment using smaller temperature intervals within that range to be confident of finding the optimum accurately.

6 You would add 1 cm³ stock solution to 7 cm³ water.

7 The gradations on a gas syringe are 1 cm³ apart, or less. This means they give it good resolution (the ability to distinguish small units), making each reading more accurate (nearer the true value) and the whole series of readings more precise (with little variation between them).

8 To ensure the colours are a valid representation, the mixtures should be heated to the same temperature for the same length of time. Unless the reaction was stopped using hydrochloric acid, the reactions in the heated tubes would continue and the colours would continue to change.

9 Its concentration is between 3% and 4%.

10 Its concentration is 3.7%.

11 You could conveniently measure the volume of gas/number of bubbles of gas released per unit time.

12 The enzyme will break down pectin at the surface of the pieces of apple tissue. Consequently, the surface area limits the rate at which enzyme–substrate complexes can form and, hence, the rate of reaction.

13 If you answered yes, your explanation would be that you could assume all 5 cm³ of enzyme in buffer solution was filtered into each preparation. If you answered no, your reason would be either that you could not assume that all 5 cm³ of enzyme in buffer solution was filtered into each preparation or that you could assume that the volume of enzyme in buffer solution filtered into each preparation was constant.

14 Probably not. Some of the oxygen produced will dissolve in the water.

15 Each pulse is caused by the contraction of the left ventricle.

16 (a) Between 0 and 2 minutes, the volume of oxygen released rose quickly from 0 cm³ to 31 cm³. After 2 minutes, the rate at which oxygen was released started to decrease and the volume eventually levelled at 42 cm³ after 8 minutes. (b) In the absence of catalase, no oxygen was released between 0 and 4 minutes. Between 4 and 16 minutes the volume of oxygen released rose from 0 cm³ to 2 cm³. It then remained at 2 cm³ until the end of the experiment at 24 minutes.

17 All the hydrogen peroxide (substrate) had been broken down.

18 If you added nothing, the volume of the mixture would be less than in the experimental group. As this would affect the concentration of solutes in the mixture, it would introduce a confounding variable.

19 No. The optimum could be any temperature between 20°C and 35°C. We would have to repeat this investigation using smaller temperature intervals between these two temperatures to find the true value of the optimum.

20 Using the mean values hides the evidence that shows younger chimpanzees use more oxygen when walking on two legs than when walking on four legs, whereas the reverse is true for older chimpanzees. This difference might be critical to our conclusion.

21 It shows the precision of the results. If the values obtained in a set of repeats are similar, the results have high precision.

22 A bar chart. The data for dominant hand are discontinuous (categoric).

23 We cannot control other variables and cannot assume a causal link.

24 Yes; the standard deviations of the means overlap.

25 If the enzyme activity did slow down, the curve would start to drop towards the x-axis. A correct answer would be that the rate of increase in enzyme activity gets less or, alternatively, that the mean enzyme activity becomes constant.

26 There are many possible answers you could correctly suggest. Light intensity might affect the air temperature, so temperature is an uncontrolled variable. Temperature will affect the rate of evaporation of water from the soil and from the plant leaves, so water availability is a second uncontrolled variable. Soil temperature might also affect the rate of decomposition in the soil, so the availability of mineral ions is a third uncontrolled variable. Finally, any of the above might affect the abundance of herbivores or parasites, which is a fourth uncontrolled variable.

27 A measuring cylinder. Although the resolution of a measuring cylinder is less than that of, say, a graduated pipette, the percentage error will be relatively small.

28 Calculate the mean for each concentration. This is the mean per minute, since the table heading is 'Volume of oxygen collected in 60 seconds/cm³'.

29 You probably answered that you would join the points with straight lines, using a sharp pencil and a ruler. The reason is that you will always gain credit for this whereas you will not if you have drawn an inappropriate curve of best fit.

30 It absorbs the carbon dioxide released by the respiring organisms in the tube B. It is included in the tube A so that both tubes are identical except for the presence of living organisms.

**31** Only glycolysis. Without oxygen as the final electron acceptor in the electron transfer chain, neither the electron transfer chain nor the Krebs cycle can occur.

**32** Boiling drives air out of the water (think of how water releases bubbles of air as it boils).

**33** Abiotic factors are physical or chemical environmental factors, such as water current or soil pH. (Biotic factors are biological factors, such as the presence of competitors or parasites.)

**34** The method in Figure 31; effectively, there are more samples made using smaller divisions of the quadrat area.

**35** She caught, marked and released 50 woodlice ($N_1$). In her second sample, she caught 40 woodlice ($N_2$), of which 10 were marked ($n$). We assume that the proportion of the total population ($X$) that she collected in her first sample is the same as the proportion of marked individuals in her second sample, i.e. $N_1/X = n/N_2$. Rearranging this equation, we find that: $X = (N_1 \times N_2)/n$, which, using our numbers, becomes $(50 \times 40)/10 = 200$ woodlice.

**36** As the distance between sampling points increases, more species are missed.

Note: page numbers in **bold** refer to defined terms.